Brasses and Brass Rubbing

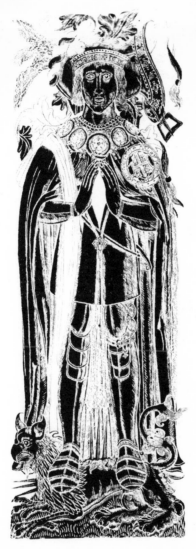

THOMAS BULLEN (BOLEYN) EARL OF WILTSHIRE, 1538
Hever, Kent

Bullen wears Garter Robes. He became an Earl and a KG largely because of his co-operation with Henry VIII over his daughter Anne Boleyn, although he lived long enough to see her executed for adultery. He became a very rich man, and was a friend of Erasmus who is known to have stayed with him at Hever Castle. After Anne's death he lived out his life in obscurity. B.L.

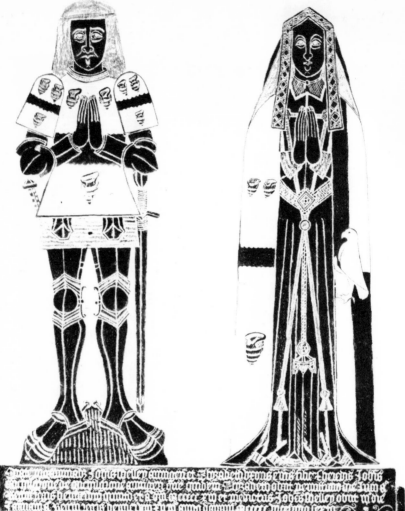
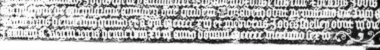

JOHN AND ELIZABETH SHELLEY, 1526
Clapham, Sussex
A good brass of its period although he is a little clumsy and she is bottle shaped. The whelk shells are the punning arms of the Shelly family. "Sable, a fess engrailed or, between 3 whelk shells argent".

He was an ancestor of Percy Bysshe Shelley, the poet.

BRASSES
AND BRASS RUBBING

SUZANNE BEEDELL

Rubbings by
Terence Cook, Suzanne Beedell, and Ginette Leach

Photographs of Rubbings and Brasses by
Suzanne Beedell

JOHN BARTHOLOMEW
Edinburgh

First published 1973
by John Bartholomew and Son Ltd.
12 Duncan Street, Edinburgh EH9 1TA
Also at 216 High Street, Bromley BR1 1PW
ISBN 0 85152 939 9

Reprinted 1978

Designed by Youé and Spooner Ltd.

Filmset by Keyspools Ltd, Golborne, Lancashire
Printed in Great Britain by
Butler and Tanner Limited, Frome, Somerset

MARGARITA CHEYNE,
1419
Hever, Kent
A lovely brass. Two angels hold
a cushion behind her head. She
was by marriage a member of the
Bullen family and a relative of
Anne Boleyn. B.L.

CONTENTS

INTRODUCTION

ABOUT THE BOOK

All brass rubbers know that visitors to churches where they are working become fascinated and want to know all about brasses and brass rubbing. Most have no idea that the brasses are even there and would not have seen them had the brass rubber not rolled back the carpets. Discussion becomes animated and searching and one ends up giving a lecture on the subject in general and thereby taking twice as long to finish the work in hand and making careless mistakes in rubbing due to disturbed concentration. But one never grudges this. My own interest in brasses was sparked off by Nicole, the teenage daughter of a Canadian friend, visiting this country, who had heard at school about brasses and insisted on doing some rubbings to take back to Canada.

I soon became an addict and began to study brasses, and I am indebted to those scholars whose brains I have picked through their books for whatever knowledge I have of the subject. A lot of specialist study into all aspects of monumental brasses has been done and carefully recorded, and more remains to be done. There are as many differing opinions as there are students; but one's opinions and approach to artistic and humanist matters are one's own. As with all works of art at all levels – and these brasses are first and foremost works of art – the eye, the imagination, the emotions, the sensibilities of the viewer decide just how important each one is personally. But however wonderful a brass may be visually, one always wants to know more about it; to understand the design, the workmanship, the techniques; to know something of the history of the individuals and their times, their dress and their personalities.

In this book I have tried, along with as many of these details as there is room for, to project something of what I feel about brasses and brass rubbings, not because what I feel is important, but to help other beginners into this totally fascinating study. I believe that churches and their contents are important not only to their members and to scholars and students, but to all of us; and if history and the continuity of life mean anything at all, there is no better way to get the feel of them than by studying and rubbing brasses in the beautiful churches of Britain.

Many books have been written about

6

brasses, some of which go far more deeply into the subject than I have room for here. Brasses are meant to be looked at, so the emphasis is on illustrations and description, together with the basic techniques of rubbing, and displaying and reproducing rubbings. For those who wish to study further, there is a full bibliography at the end of the book. My thanks and acknowledgments are due to their authors for their help in matters of fact.

ABOUT THE ILLUSTRATIONS

It takes a lot of time to amass a big collection of brass rubbings. It would take years to rub even a few hundred of the best and most interesting brasses needed for a fully representative collection, or even to photograph the brasses in situ, unless one could do nothing else. Few of us have that freedom from home or work to spare the time, so to put together enough illustrations for a book such as this is difficult, unless one uses photographs supplied by the great collections, for instance in the Victoria and Albert Museum and the British Museum. I wanted these illustrations to be made from rubbings done by those who have approached the subject as amateurs, not as scholars; so that readers will know that they too can get comparable results. For the same reasons, I have taken all the photographs myself, at home and not in studio conditions; or in churches, without the use of complicated equipment.

Many of the rubbings were done by myself and Ginette Leach, but our collection was neither big nor comprehensive. I have, however, been extremely fortunate to have Mr. Terence Cook's permission to photograph his splendid collection of rubbings, without which the book would not have been possible for at least another five years. The difference in our techniques, both in rubbing and finishing, are noticeable, and I think interesting. Mr.

Cook's rubbings are marked T.C., mine and Mrs. Leach's B.L.

It would have been possible to touch up both rubbings and photographs so that the illustrations were without a single blemish, without a wobbly line or a white spot and completely without texture; but brass rubbings never look like that. Some brasses are easier to rub than others; one works better some days than others; some brasses photograph better than others. These variations are noticeable throughout the illustrations. I am not apologising for these variations, just saying that they do truly represent the rubbings and the brasses as they are, and they represent the kind of results you should be able to achieve. If I may make an analogy; the illustrations in cookery books look absolutely marvellous, but when you cook the same dishes at home they never look anything like so splendid, although they may taste delicious!

There are omissions; with several thousand brasses to choose from it would be surprising if many fine brasses were not left out; again we have been limited by force of circumstances. Mr. Cook and I have concentrated on rubbing brasses in churches which we could reach from our homes without travelling hundreds of miles. Neither of us have made specialist studies of any particular aspect of monumental brasses, so when visiting a church for only a few hours, we have tended to rub the finest brasses or the ones which appealed to us personally. Nevertheless, I think our joint collections are fairly representative of all types, and of course there are many more brasses just as fine as those illustrated here for you to seek out and rub for yourselves.

AN APPROACH TO BRASS RUBBING

A church has two main functions; it is a place of worship and a storehouse of history. Enter a church and one is immediately aware of its sanctity; a place apart where man worships his God in continuity with worshippers of the past and future. It does not matter in the least what your own religious beliefs are or if you have none, it is the power of the faith of others that is impressive.

Since its beginning, every church has steadily accumulated on paper, in stone, in glass and in brass, the historical records of its users; brief notes on lives as long or as short as yours and mine. "Rest in Peace" is a comparatively modern postscript to life; the pre-reformation generations asked you to "pray for their souls". If their souls existed then to be prayed for, they exist now, and so one is again instantly involved with the past. In any case the men and women commemorated on those brasses are all our ancestors. Allowing four generations a century, and going back to the fourteen hundreds, that makes twenty generations. Therefore twenty generations ago one had well over a million grandparents. The population of the country at that time was tiny, so any of those characters (except the officially celibate ecclesiastics!) could be your grandparents far removed.

The point I am trying to make is that too often the contents of our churches are regarded by antiquarians and archaeologists as things from which the general public should be divided by ropes and glass cases, and which are properly only to be studied by the expert. Arising in the first place from attempts to prevent wilful damage, this attitude tends to widen the gap between church and people. The antiquarians treasure the brasses and other memorials for their antiquarian, historical or aesthetic qualities, and forget their meaning in simple human terms. Others come to revere them as if they were holy images, sacred in themselves or consecrated by their relationship with the dead, and to see brass rubbing as sacreligious or at least disrespectful.

It is so obvious that it barely needs saying that all these monuments should be cherished and protected because they are irreplaceable, and unique historical social and artistic records, and because they are memorials to the dead whom we respect whether they died last week or five centuries ago. But for me it also goes without saying that access to the brasses for any non-destructive purpose should not be denied to anyone, and that to say that the brass rubber, even for commercial purposes, is committing spiritual trespass is rubbish. Most churches charge a fee for brass rubbing, the money going towards the upkeep of the church. Whether or not it is wrong for money to change hands at any stage over brass rubbings could be argued for ever and the purists do have a point when they say that it should be stopped altogether because it is commercialised all along the line; if only because commercialisation encourages over-rubbing and the possibility of damage, very slight though that possibility is.

Yet brass rubbing remains one of the few ways, perhaps the only way, in which those who cannot create works of art for themselves can recreate them without needing enormous talent or years of training. The very fact of having to go into churches to do it has brought many people into contact with beauty and history in many forms, and above all into contact with religious faith perhaps for the first time. One would have to be cynical indeed to gain nothing but callouses from hours spent on one's knees in a church, rubbing brasses. If the problem of the church today is to draw people through its many doors and if pop groups, drama, flower festivals and the like are used to solve it, then what on earth is wrong with brass rubbing? Fortunate is the church which contains a good brass. There is a continual stream of people only too happy to pay for the privilege of taking rubbings from it. It does put extra work on the clergy and their helpers to keep an eye on things, make appointments, etc. I am sure that 99 per cent of rubbers do not abuse the privilege. The few who do, usually through ignorance and thoughtlessness, are just as likely to be brought to order by other brass rubbers who wish to be able to continue their peaceful and fascinating work without opposition.

It has been pointed out that a thing of beauty is not made less beautiful by being reproduced, yet to see the same work of art reproduced again and again renders it tedious. One would not have more than one rubbing of the same brass on display at the same time, and there is as much satisfaction in having a fine rubbing in the house as in having a fine print of a great picture. It would be wonderful to possess the picture, or the brass itself, but that is not possible, and second best has to be good enough. Does this make one wallpaper-minded over brass rubbings? I doubt it. If, by any extraordinary chance, someone laid down a memorial brass to me, and in five hundred years' time other people decided that it would be nice to have me on their walls, I should feel nothing but complimented. Surely the purpose of a memorial is to perpetuate the memory of the dead, and surely our monumental brasses have achieved their purpose in the most spectacular way. Thomas and Margaret de Freville *(fig. 1)* and the rest could not have dreamed, five hundred years ago, that their brasses would bring them even such a measure of immortality and that their names would be familiar to thousands of members of a generation that has landed armoured men upon the moon!

1 THOMAS AND MARGARET DE FREVILLE, 1410
Little Shelford, Cambridgeshire
One of the most beautiful brasses of its period. The pose is completely natural, with the two figures turned towards each other, holding hands. Thomas's left hand rests comfortably on his baudric and Margaret's upon her breast. Even the dog looks upwards affectionately towards his master. Margaret wears a wimple covering her throat which indicates that she was a widow. There is another brass of the same date in this church to Robert de Freville and his wife. The pose and the lady's dress are slightly different but the knight is almost identical. Certainly the same engraver did both brasses. T.C.

9

THE BRASSES

A BRIEF HISTORY OF MONUMENTAL BRASSES

The geographical isolation of Great Britain during the Middle Ages, when Europe was developing away from the Dark Ages, through the Gothic period into the Renaissance, affected the development of all our cultures. Although Britain is part of Europe, its people, its arts and customs, its manners and its attitudes are not and never have been identical with those of continental Europe. Populated by successive waves of invaders from Scandinavia to the Mediterranean, Britain assimilated and subtly changed them all. The early Catholic faith took a very firm hold on this country and, from Saxon times to the Reformation, our parish churches were built in their thousands and became centres of community life. The churches themselves were built in architectural styles which owed much to European influences but which were and are unmistakably British and unique. All our art forms have a simplicity which owes a lot to our insularity. Cultural changes, ideas and fashions were slow to cross the channel and our artists were able to develop with much less interference from these things

than were European artists.

The social systems were such that each local lord of the manor dominated the village and the church, and when he died, in peace or war, he was commemorated in his local abbey, cathedral or village church, according to his status, usually near his home, however remote. Up to the thirteenth century, stone and marble memorials, mostly recumbent statues lying in probably totally uncharacteristic poses of religious repose, were the usual form of memorial *(fig. 9)*. But even then it must have been obvious that the older statues were wearing badly, were liable to damage and were not going to be the almost eternal memorials their owners looked for. Also, they must have realised that not many generations could go on putting large pieces of statuary in churches without filling every available space. Therefore, when the new material, brass, latten or laten, as it was then called, became available, it very quickly became extremely popular. Memorial engravings on brass plate seemed infinitely more durable, and have proved so to be. In the flat, they took up no room in the churches and could even be walked upon without apparent damage. They were no more expensive than marble or stone and, although transport was difficult and costly for anything of any size in those days, brass plates and their stone casements must have been a little easier to carry for long distances than stone or marble statues.

Until Elizabethan times, it was necessary to import the brass sheets, because they were only made on the continent, mostly near Cologne on the Rhine. It was often referred to as cullen plate. The alloy was approximately two-thirds copper and one-third zinc, with a little lead and tin. There were big copper deposits in the Hartz mountains, and calamine ore – zinc carbonate – came from Aachen. The calamine ore was ground up and mixed with charcoal and small pieces of copper. This was heated enough to distil out the zinc but not enough to melt the copper. The volatile zinc permeated the copper and formed brass. The brass was then heated and poured into moulds to form plates between three and five millimetres thick. These plates were later hammered out and the surface planished by hammering before the engravings were begun. The plates were between two feet six inches and three feet square. Some of the pitting on brass plates is due to the air bubbles trapped during the smelting process which have become exposed as the brass wore down. Most surface blemishes are due to the hobnailed boots and tramping feet of centuries. Usually the monumental brasses were made up by engraving several plates and laying them side by side; occasionally the plates were brazed together to form a single sheet before engraving. When one comes across a brass which has a large area missing, it is usually a whole plate which has gone, and the plate joins are very clearly visible on many brasses and brass rubbings (*fig. 2*).

The engravers had to be very careful to match up their work on successive plates.

There is a very obvious error on the brass of Sir Robert de Septvans. Where the top plate butts with the middle plate, the handle of the winnowing fan on the shield does not match up. The engraver made a mess of the left gauntlet, although it was at that point that he realised his error and put

2 SIR JOHN DE NORTHWOOD, 1330
Minster, Sheppy, Kent
Detail. Some of the lower half of this figure is restoration work, probably French. A narrow plate can quite clearly be seen where it has been inserted across the shield where it replaced a damaged or missing part. The engraving is extremely well matched, but it has been done slightly more neatly, especially the cross-hatching. The original cross-hatching was probably there to make a key for paint or enamel, so it was not done so carefully as the later work done purely to match up the areas. T.C.

3 SIR ROBERT DE SEPTVANS, 1306
Chartham, Kent
Detail. The engraver's error on the handle of
the winnowing fan and the left gauntlet
shows clearly. B.L.

things right across the rest of the join (fig. 3).

By the end of the sixteenth century brass was being made in this country. The alloy was a little different and the plates were rolled, not cast. Copper plates were made, then the whole plates fired in the presence of zinc to turn it into brass. These plates were a brighter yellow, but were thinner, softer and more easy to dent and damage than the old cullen plates.

To return to the early days when all the heavy brass sheets were made in Europe. The whole conception and art of engraving plates began in Europe, particularly in Flanders, and all the earliest brasses – rectangular sheets engraved with huge complex designs – were done there. Enough remain to give us a taste of what a glory they once were, but the wars and avarice of centuries have reduced them to a handful out of thousands. Quite a lot of finished brasses were imported here complete with their stone casements, but they must have been very expensive and rare things (fig. 53). A few brasses of Flemish workmanship have survived here, but after 1560 many were turned over and re-used (see page 56, Palimpsests).

One gets the definite feeling that after the first years the continental style just did not catch on here, and that both buyers and producers preferred the English styles which were developing quickly. There is little difference between an inscription engraved in stone and in brass, except that the latter is much more durable. The two arts probably developed side by side, but there is all the difference in the world between the Flemish style of picture engraved on plate, and silhouette set in stone of the English style, which took over during the thirteenth and fourteenth centuries. So it was the brass plates which were brought here slowly and laboriously, first by horse and cart, or perhaps down river by boat, then by boat across the channel and the North Sea, and again by horse and cart to the engravers' workshops, and by horse and cart yet again to the churches. In our days of rapid transport and mechanisation when no one heaves weights like these around by hand, it is hard to visualise it all: loaded carts pulled by sweating horses along muddy or stony roads; the often very dangerous and difficult sea crossings; the harbours which were little more than sheltered bays. In fact from what records remain, we find that transport costs were very high; between a third and a fifth of the totals.

The earliest English brasses dated from about 1275, and by 1300 big military brasses were being made, several of which survive (figs. 4, 17, 18, 19). Probably just as many ecclesiastical brasses were made, but were later destroyed (see page 23). Only the indents now remain (fig. 16). There are indents of big ecclesiastical brasses in the floor of the Martydom in Canterbury Cathedral, tantalising reminders of what once there were. In 1348 the Black Death swept Britain and wiped out half the population. Probably very few brasses were made during those years which, in all kinds of ways, altered the courses of history and art. By the end of the fourteenth century the work was again in full swing, and there were schools of engravers in London and several provincial centres all on the eastern side of the country, near to the ports where the sheets of metal could be brought from the continent. Here again, the difficulty and cost of transport governed the location of the centres, and the distribution of brasses through Britain emphasises the fact. The southern, eastern and home counties had most brasses, and this is where most of the survivors are. There were probably two workshops in London, possibly one in York and certainly one in Norwich (Norfolk still has many splendid brasses). Other engravers' workshops were in

4 SIR JOHN D'AUBERNON, 1277
Stoke Dabernon, Surrey
The earliest surviving brass in England. His
arms borne on the flat shield are "azure, a
chevron or" and the blue enamel has also
survived. Note the stitching on the sword
belt so clearly shown, and the decoration on
genouilleres and guige. Sir John's tough
dominant face looks you straight in the eye
across the centuries, even though the left
shoulder strap of his surcoat, like the Venus
de Milo's draperies, seems irretrievably to
have slipped. T.C.

Ipswich and Cambridge and Bristol in the
west country and Coventry in the Mid-
lands also had small workshops. Other
engravers in provincial centres, gold-
smiths, bell founders and local metal
workers all turned out monumental
brasses and the quality of their work is very
variable, according to the ability and
techniques of the engraver. As time went
by, local craftsmen turned out small
brasses of very uninspired and stereotyped
design. Students of brasses have been able,
by comparing details, to link up brasses in
different churches and state that they were
probably done in the same workshop or
by the same hand. When you first go brass
rubbing or looking at brasses you soon
discover similarities which make you feel
certain that the same engraver has been at
work, especially as you are probably looking in one area to begin with. This is one
of the most exciting and interesting aspects
of brass study, a kind of detective work,
and you may easily come up with similarities that no one else has spotted.

At the beginning of the fifteenth century
the great Gothic themes of design still pre-
dominated and this was the finest period
of monumental brasses *(fig. 5)*. As the
Renaissance, much more naturalistic in
concept, swept Europe, the splendid,
simple designs became unfashionable and,
except in a few cases, the Renaissance styles
did not produce such aesthetically satisfy-
ing brasses. However, very many appealing and naïve brasses date from the period
1500–1540 *(fig. 6)* perhaps a period when
brass design was at its worst. Then came
the Reformation and the whole emphasis
and position of the church changed. Many
brasses were destroyed *(see page 23)* and
one can only assume that there was not
much future in being an engraver of church
brasses. The thinner British brass was
being made and this affected techniques.
Small rectangular plates, more like cartoons than works of art, became popular

14

5 PETER AND ELIZABETH HALLE,
1430
Herne, Kent
This fine pair, hand in hand, but lacking the
naturalistic pose of the De Frevilles *(fig. 1)*
were contemporary with Henry V who died
aged 34 in 1422. They must have lived
through a glittering period of English

history, only to see the beginnings of decline
in their last years under Henry VI. Peter
Halle's armour is typical of the period and is a
fine example. There are several other brasses
in the area showing almost identical armour,
presumably worked by the same engraver.
Head-dress, jewellery and styling of the kirtle
are especially attractive, as is the long coated
dog. B.L.

Off your charite pray for the Soules of Thomas manfeld esquyer
and Agnes his wyf one of the daughters & heyers of John Gebon
Wall of ... in the Counten of Kent gentilmā ...
of ... now late wedow of ... Thomas manfeld whiche & Thomas
... the ... day of august an dni ... on whons sowl god haue mcy

**6 THOMAS MANFELD AND HIS
WIVES**, 1540
Taplow, Buckinghamshire
A clumsy brass, typical of the worst of the
period. It is naïve enough to be quite
appealing, and the details of costume and
armour and head-dress are clear. The
inscription in English asks that of your
charity you pray for their souls. T.C.

16

7 ROBERT BULKELEY, 1556
Cople, Bedfordshire
A badly drawn, over-decorated,
out-of-perspective rectangular plate. T.C.

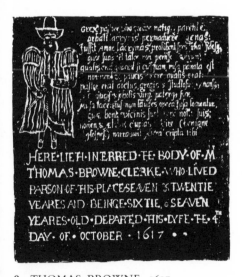

8 THOMAS BROWNE, 1617
Piddlehinton, Dorset
A terrible example of the rectangular plate,
with a poem, and inscription which is self
explanatory. The figure can only be
described as a doodle! T.C.

and economic depression meant that people went for cheaper memorials; the brass plates could be mounted without expensive stone casements *(fig. 7)*.

Queen Elizabeth did much by edict to halt the ravages of her predecessors as far as the Church of England was concerned, and brasses again became popular. The better brasses of this late period were fine works of art in their very different way. By the middle of the seventeenth century the whole art, apart from inscriptions, died out. There are some fine inscriptions *(see page 64)* remaining from this period and, right up to the present day, brass plates bearing inscriptions remain popular *(see fig. 8)*.

In modern times there have been a few attempts to make monumental brasses, but their quality is as different from that of the great early brasses as is the quality of Victorian parish churches from that of the pre-Reformation ones.

ENGRAVING TECHNIQUES AND FIXING

The artists' designs were transferred to the brass with chalk or black paint, and the engraver set to work with hammer and engravers' burin, a tool which cut a V-shaped notch. In some cases, large areas of surface were cut away to leave the carving in relief, but generally the lines of the drawing were chiselled out. Many inscriptions are cut wide and deep, much wider than the lines of the figures. This makes the rubbing of inscriptions very difficult, as the paper tends to press down into wide cut areas. Shields with heraldic charges were also cut this way, and the areas cross-hatched to make a key for paint or enamel. The later brasses on thin rolled English brass were lightly cut, and some were actually etched with acid.

Many early brasses were coloured in with paint or enamel, and must have been splendid to see. Little colour has survived because through the centuries it has cracked away, being much less durable than brass. Yet it can still be seen quite clearly in the crevices of some brasses, and the shield of Sir John d'Aubernon still bears a lot of its blue enamel (fig. 4).

The brasses were fixed to their indents by being laid in pitch and riveted into sockets cut into the stone matrix. These sockets were filled with lead, and the rivets set into them before the metal hardened so that they stuck up from the base. Corresponding holes were then drilled in the brass, which was set into the bitumen filled matrix with the rivets protruding through the drilled holes. The rivets were then cut down and hammered over to hold the brass in position. Many empty indents still have the bottoms of the rivets firmly in position, proof of the fact that the brasses were hacked up bodily, and that the workmen who set them in place did their jobs well enough to last for centuries, provided no one interfered (fig. 16).

Rivets were set with little care for the look of the brass. It is quite usual to find a rivet in the middle of someone's face, or breaking the most important and sweeping line of an engraving, when it would seem that with a little more care they could have been put where they would have blended in without being noticeable.

DESIGN

Mankind has always wished to commemorate its dead and to build its own memorials before death; it is one way of grasping at immortality. To be absolutely certain that your memorial is worthy of you and that your descendants have not skimped on it and you, it is necessary to supervise its construction before you die, and this was quite common practice as the written records we have make quite clear. Life was short in those days, and many women died in childbirth, so quite often a bereaved husband would have his own brass made at the same time as that of his first wife, with a space left on the inscription plate for his own details to be added, although this was often not done by the survivors (fig. 36). Sir John de Cobham, who rebuilt the church in which he lies and holds a model of it to prove the fact for all time, had his brass made in about 1364, although he did not die until 1407.

It is believed that Sir Robert de Septvans' brass was commissioned and laid after his death by his son. Another very famous brass, that of King Ethelred of Wessex who died in 873, was not made until 1440, as long a span of time as has elapsed to the present day since the fourteenth century brasses were made. It was rather as if we should now decide to lay a commemorative brass to the Black Prince or Henry V.

While the designs were probably drawn to specification by hired artists and not by the engravers themselves (at any rate the bigger and better brasses), the similarities between the figures in each period make it probable that only comparatively few designers and engravers were working at one and the same time. As the art became popular, stock figures were used for the lesser brasses on which only small details and inscriptions differed. In some cases where more than one wife is shown (even on better brasses) they are almost identical (figs. 6 and 73).

Inscriptions are a different matter, as today these would have been dictated, even composed, by the customer, some of them in extremely bad Latin. Archbishop Harsnett (fig. 51), bishop successively of Chichester, Norwich and York, wrote his own epitaph, a fact which someone who obviously thought he was too modest, pointed out in an additional inscription.

The Flemish brasses were rectangular plates, but the British taste demanded cut-out figures, surrounded by fillets bearing inscriptions and later with ornate gothic canopies. It is this single fact which makes our brasses so impressive. The cut-out figures, deeply engraved, set into stone casements, have far greater impact on the eye than the ornately engraved rectangular plates. These latter are very fine and often richly beautiful, but the viewer must stop and consider them and study long. Only one look at the simpler British brasses is enough to make a lasting impression. Their elegant artistry is obvious. These figures of men, women and children, set in stone strike one immediately as just that, human beings who once lived as we live, however stylized or disproportionate they may sometimes be; they are totally poignant in their humanity. The rectangular brasses just don't have this kind of impact. The earlier brasses made in this country were big, life size or bigger, with great canopies around them, which again gives them terrific strength. The Flemish engraved plates were also very big. The governing factor was probably that, early on, only the really wealthy could afford monumental brasses or even knew about them. They were perhaps a status symbol, and it would seem more logical to have a big brass than a small one. As the years passed and everyone who was anyone had a brass, they became smaller to fit smaller and smaller purses.

When you study brasses it soon becomes apparent how the styles changed for better and worse, and how they were linked with the great artistic and social movements of the times. As in any form of art, there was within the limitations of definite styles the odd genius who produced great works of art; there were a lot of first-rate designers and engravers, and some downright bad ones. The less beautiful brasses do have a curious attraction about them, even to the extent of being to our eyes funny. So often there is some feature of a brass which strikes one with particular poignancy, and part of the pleasure of brass rubbing is that

one begins to speculate, to wonder about the details of the brass. Was that necklace a special gift from husband to wife? Was that dog a particularly faithful companion? How did they feel about the premature deaths of all those children? What killed them, plague, measles, appendicitis? Were they really so elegant and splendid or was it just the flattery of an artist trying to please a client?

There is a school of thought which believes that these brasses were in no way attempts at portraiture, neither facially nor in fact of costume, armour, pets and so on. One just ordered a brass of a certain type, supplied heraldic details and dates and specified the type of dress but not its detail. Maybe this is true to some extent, but undoubtedly some of the brasses are portraits and some of the costumes personal. There was no technical reason why an engraver could not reproduce a personal feature if requested, and the tools and materials were flexible enough in expert hands to allow exact renderings of whatever the artist wanted. The hand that engraved the hooked lines to indicate the folds of Lady de Creke's dress (fig. 25) was perfectly capable of making the face a simple portrait, and it would seem illogical to spend time and trouble working on small details of fancy decoration and to save it by cutting faces which bore no resemblance to their owners.

Gothic art forms and ideas were still persisting, but just beginning to decline before the tremendous overwhelming waves of the Renaissance when the first surviving brasses were made, so artistically a period of transition was beginning. The early knights are splendidly naturalistic, reflecting this movement away from the Gothic themes which had produced most of the majestic cathedrals of Europe. The folds of the surcoats, the relaxed crossed legs, the curly hair all rather belie the hands folded in prayer and the pillowed heads and feet, a hangover from the style of the three-dimensional monuments of wood and stone *(fig. 9)* which lay above the older tombs. Brasses also lay on tombs, and the figures were meant to be reclining; yet one feels that the men are in fact standing up, especially Sir John d'Aubernon whose legs are not crossed *(fig. 4)*, and about to assume the more belligerent pose with hand on sword hilt. For a while an even more relaxed pose became popular and men and women stand with one hip slightly stuck out almost like a modern model. Sir John d'Aubernon the Younger *(fig. 10)* and Sir John de Cobham 2nd baronet *(fig. 11)* are almost S-shaped and do not have crossed legs, and in the eye of their artists were surely never recumbent, although their hands still pray and their feet still rest on lions. The impression is that they are actually standing on the beasts! The canopies carefully framed the figures and much care was taken to keep the proportions right. The canopies echoed the architectural styles of the English parish churches, developing from Decorated to Perpendicular and becoming more and more complex and splended. Architects had long discovered the Golden Section, a rule of proportion which decrees that the ratio of the height of an arch to the height of the shafts is as of the height of the shafts (or pillars) to the total height. Later on this rule was ignored and attempts at perspective produced a far less satisfactory balance.

Then the S-bend was abandoned, there was a reaction towards stylisation, and realism was forgotten. The knights and their ladies stood bolt upright, on stiff legs, or lay flat in the same unnatural pose if you see them that way. Men and women appear to be exactly the same heights, the men made taller only by their pointed bascinets. Yet this period is outstanding, and the simplicity of line of the best brasses is magnificent. The gentle curves of the knights' outlines and the straight lines of

9 SIR JOHN DE SEPTVANS, 1458
Ash-next-Sandwich, Kent
A descendant of Sir Robert de Septvans. He wears transitional armour with mail aventail. The details of armour and pose show clearly and it is easy to see how the engravers of brasses tried to follow this pose. Sir John's head rests upon his great helm with its fish crest, here supported by a reclining angel, unfortunately headless. He wears the SS collar of the Lancastrians, and his misericord is by his side. His feet rest upon a lion which looks back towards him. This shows quite clearly how the engravers turned the lion on the flat brasses to an unnatural position from what was perfectly natural on a three-dimensional effigy. His wife, Katherine, lies beyond him, but only her hands can be seen here.

their armour and swords contrasting superbly with the flowing curves of the women's dresses and head-dresses. The ecclesiastics too have splendid stylised vestments with much clean cut decoration, and the civilians are neat and tidy in their bag sleeves and straight folds. Perhaps the abiding impression of this period is one of style and neatness; simple clean lines and no fuss. Factors which in any age add up to elegance. Not immortal works of art, but very good design indeed. That these people could have been so elegant in real life is most unlikely; it was the eye of the artist that made them so *(fig. 12)*.

By this time the Renaissance was in full swing and its ideas becoming really influential. Realism became all important again, and from the middle of the fifteenth century the artists and engravers were trying to cope with a style which was neither easy to work two dimensionally nor which allowed for simplicity in engraving. To try to reproduce shapes which could only be seen properly in profile, to indicate fine details and perspectives which needed shading, was too difficult on flat plates using the techniques and tools of the time, and most of the beauty was lost. The fine brass of Christina Phelyp *(fig. 13)* shows clearly what happens when you try to be realistic.

In this case the design was partly successful, but in many brasses it was not, and merely resulted in distorted poses. The figures made no pretence at all at lying down. The whole art went through a difficult period and brasses became completely different in style. Instead of the tremendous sweeping lines and curves of the earlier brasses, with little shading or detail, the engravers began to cover the whole surface of the plates with cross hatching to represent fur, material and shading and to include all kinds of details, such as tiled floors and even scenes. Small rectangular plates like cartoons *(fig. 7)*

10 SIR JOHN D'AUBERNON THE YOUNGER, 1327
Stoke Dabernon, Surrey. T.C.

11 JOHN DE COBHAM, 2nd Baron,
1354
Cobham, Kent
The inscription reads: "You who pass round
this place, pray for the soul of the courteous
host called John de Cobham. May God grant
him entire pardon. He died the day after the
feast of St. Matthew and the Almighty took
him to Himself in the year of Grace 1354 and
cast down his mortal enemies." Laid at the
same time as the brass of the 3rd Baronet, the
family obviously decided to make a job of
their memorials while they were at it.
Perhaps the engraver charged less for two
commissions executed at the same time. T.C.

12 JOHN PERYENT and his wife JOAN
RISEYN, 1415
Digswell, Hertfordshire
An elegant pair. Joan Peryent is unusual; her
head-dress is unique as are the swan on her
collar and the hedgehog at her feet. This pair
moved in the highest circles as he was Esquire
for the Body successively to Richard II,
Henry IV and Henry V, and Master of Horse
to Queen Joanna of Navarre. Both wear the
Lancastrian SS collar. The design is very
beautiful, but just a little stiff. T.C.

22

13 CHRISTINA PHELYP, 1470
Herne, Kent
Wife of Matthew Phelyp, Lord Mayor of
London and Goldsmith to Henry VIII.
Although this brass is damaged it is still very
impressive. The missing part of the mantle
was probably a different alloy, maybe stolen
at some time for its value. The head-dress is
very exaggerated *(see page 44 and fig. 45)*.
The hand pose is unusual but appears
occasionally on brasses made in East Anglia,
and is probably an alternative hand attitude of
prayer. In this brass the hands held up and
facing forward appear to spring like little
wings from her breasts, without arms, which
are totally foreshortened and only indicated
by part of the cuffs. The inscription which is
not shown here *(figs. 74 and 75)* is unusual in
that the letters are not engraved, but in relief.
B.L.

became popular and the cut-out figures
seem to be much more obviously attempts
at personal portraits than they ever were in
the early days; when the emphasis was on
armour, costume, heraldry and rank,
rather than on feature. From the middle
sixteenth century on, the subjects are
recognisable first as individuals. There is
something much more comfortable about
the later brasses, especially those of
women. Perhaps the sadness or humour
of many of the expressions was in fact
accidental, but they are certainly more
recognisable as personalities rather than
images. The women are shorter and fatter,
the men have distinctive hair cuts,
moustaches and beards *(fig. 14)*.

The early Tudor brasses around the first
half of the sixteenth century show these
changes clearly, the shading being mostly
clumsy and bearing little relation to the
realities of light and shade. Design for its
own sake became extinct for a while
(fig. 15). The total change of style which
followed the manufacture of brass in this
country, when it became possible to
engrave very fine lines and all kinds of
shading, led to a totally realistic style in
which brasses became more like drawings
in late tudor times. The late sixteenth
century artists and engravers did master
their medium again and some of the
brasses are finely drawn, designed and
executed, so that the art had a final fling,
but it never reached the heights of the first
two hundred and fifty years. There were a
few brasses, very variable in quality, made
in Carolian times, when, except for inscriptions, it petered out altogether.

LOST AND DAMAGED BRASSES

When those mediaeval gentry ordered
their monumental brasses they must have
thought that they were buying almost
indestructible memorials; not only because the brass was so tough, but because

the world they lived in was, in their terms, stable. In Britain at any rate, successful invasion by pagan foreigners would have seemed to them to be the only possible chance of destruction. Surely, they must have reasoned, this will not happen, and who else would dream or dare to remove or damage or destroy their brasses, enshrined in the churches of the universal Catholic faith. No great changes, except in art and fashion took place, certainly technical progress was slow, and how was it possible to envisage any change in ways of transport or communication? In the twentieth century it is not difficult to believe that in five hundred years' time the world may be unrecognisably different. In the fifteenth century the horse and sailing boat were the fastest means of getting goods and messages around, and the steam or internal combustion engine and radio unimaginable. That the power of the Roman Catholic Church should ever be overthrown must also have been unthinkable.

Yet it came to pass. When, in the six-

14 JANE BARNE, 1609
Willesden, Middlesex
Surely a portrait; this dumpy little woman in her farthingale and ruff is a far cry from the lissom creatures of the fourteenth and fifteenth centuries. This rubbing is in silver on black paper. The brass was clumsily engraved, and the plate is badly pitted. T.C.

15 THOMAS INGEHAM and his wife ELIZABETH, 1559
Goodnestone-next-Wingham, Kent
A clumsy, inelegant, but not unpleasing brass, a little damaged. The inscription, which begins: "By doleful dint of deaths dire dart" records that they died young, within a day or two of each other. Armour and dress of the period show very clearly.

24

teenth century, Henry VIII and his Reformation brought about wholesale destruction of the great abbeys, his minister and agent Thomas Cromwell (a bad name for brasses) plundered from them everything of value. Westminster Abbey and St. Albans still have a few brasses left, but obviously all the other great abbeys must have had dozens of magnificent memorials, for where else more likely than the great monastic churches would many great men have wished to be buried and to have their memorials? Some were removed in time and saved, others were reused for different purposes and fragments of these have been rediscovered; but most went, melted down for sheer profit. During the short reign of Henry's son and successor Edward VI, the spirit of the country was still iconoclastic, and many more brasses were removed from parish churches. By edict all traces of Catholic style of worship had to be removed, and because brasses were valuable, whereas stone memorials were not, plenty of people took advantage of this edict to make a legitimate profit. Any part of the brass with direct religious significance was particularly at risk. Trinities, crosses, saints, angels, prayer scrolls, even engraved prayers could be wrenched up without anyone being able to protest. There are plenty of brasses which have survived with prayers defaced *(fig. 68)* and although we find this frightful enough, at least they were lucky to survive at all.

By the strange twists of history, there followed the reign of Catholic Mary which stopped a lot of the church wrecking that was going on, but when Protestant Elizabeth came to the throne, many Protestants felt that they could again take advantage and make a profit out of what brasses were left. Luckily Elizabeth was for her times an enlightened woman, and a sensible and extremely crafty one. Never knowing which way the cat might jump, she always played both options, and determined to maintain a tolerant balance wherever she could (although what passed for tolerance in those days might seem more like tyranny now). She issued edicts strictly forbidding any damage or mutilation of monuments to the dead; and this did halt the wholesale destruction. At the same time, the practice of having brass memorials made had never ceased, and although after the Reformation most contained no figures or words of purely religious significance, the supply was steadily being replenished. Powerful landowners and squires took good care to see that the memorials and those of their ancestors were no further damaged. Elizabeth's edicts even demanded the restoration and repair of damaged monuments, but not a lot was done. It was obvious to the politically acute that more religious trouble was in store in Britain, and some brasses were laid in out-of-the-way places with this in mind. One example of this is the brass of Archbishop Harsnett of York *(fig. 51)*. He had it laid at Chigwell, Essex were he had once been vicar. The brass is an inch thick and was riveted immensely strongly right through the stone. When the Civil War came and the brasses of York Minster were ravaged he just was not there.

The second Cromwell, Oliver the Puritan, went after the brass for munitions and money, and he concentrated his efforts where pickings were easiest. It is on record that the Cromwellians stripped York and Lincoln Minsters of 200 brasses each. The Royalists took quite a few for munitions as well, and between them they almost cleared what must have been the finest brasses of all, those in the great cathedrals. The tragedy is that, had these been left, they would probably have escaped the later ravages.

In the seventeenth century, a time when church finances were at a low ebb, the churchwardens ripped up brasses to sell for their scrap value. The final tragedy was so near to our own time that it is almost the worst of all. The Victorians, full of zeal and bad taste, decided to restore and to alter the parish churches of England. Chancel floors, where lay many brasses which had survived all the other disasters, offended the Victorians by being paved with worn stone. So they pulled them up and laid the terrible tiles which still remain in so many places. If the brasses were kept at all, they were thrown loose with other odds and ends into scrap boxes in the vestry. At best they were relaid in odd corners or put up on walls, and only occasionally in the chancels. Great big church organs were installed and if the brasses were in the way, they were either covered over or removed; other exten-sions and alterations took no regard of the brasses. It may seem odd that in view of the fact that there were once literally thousands and thousands of brasses, although empty indents and matrices are common *(fig. 16)*, there are not more of them from which one could trace missing brasses. Those too were removed or filled in, in the cause of tidiness.

One wonders how many indents or even brasses themselves lie hidden still to be discovered. In some cases, tiles were laid on top of existing paving and, although it seems unlikely that the brasses were left, and more likely that they were pulled up and sold to pay for the tiles, yet a feeling of respect for the dead and their living descendants may have prevailed in some cases and the brasses covered but not removed. Who knows, maybe one day

16 INDENT
Eastry, Kent
An empty indent with more than twenty rivets, the lower halves of which are still firmly in position. Typical of the lost brass. Probably not, in this case an important or beautiful one, but nevertheless gone for ever.

the tiles will be taken up and untold treasures revealed. Certainly there should be many filled-in indents.

Robbery, damage and mistreatment still continue. Small brasses, shields, inscriptions and so on still disappear. Damaged and loose brasses are not properly replaced or repaired. Polishers are allowed a free hand. I found a parish church recently with small brasses which had been taken up and mounted on wooden panels; the broken parts of the figures were not even correctly matched and the brasses brilliant. I remonstrated, and the vicar's wife said that the church cleaners took great pride in the polish on the brasses. In other cases, clear plastic has been poured over brasses to protect them from rubbers, which seems a drastic and final treatment.

Luckily, there are some specialists in restoring and refixing brasses in the traditional way without damage or alteration, and with the permission of diosecan authorities this work is being carried out.

17 SIR ROBERT DE SEPTVANS, 1306
Chartham, Kent

This man was a contemporary of Edward I, Longshanks, the tall and spendid king whose motto was "to each his own" and who was animated by a passionate regard for justice and law. The great crusades were over and except for a few sporadic forays, not concerning western Europe at that time, so Sir Robert probably never went crusading. So much for the theory that crossed legs indicate crusaders.

Sir Robert was a member of a Kentish family which has only recently become extinct, there being memorials in brass and stone all over the county, especially in Ash by Sandwich church, right up to the 17th century.

The arms on the shield are "Azure, 3 winnowing fans Or" The surcoat is "semee (sprinkled) with winnowing fans. These arms are a pun on the name 'Septvans' – seven fans, and he displays seven on his surcoat. His motto continued the theme and was 'Dissipabo inimicos Regis mei, ut paleam' – 'The enemies of my King, I will disperse like chaff''.

Sir Robert died aged 57 and the brass was probably commissioned by his son and engraved about 1320. The head of the lion has been missing for three hundred years. In spite of its slight mistakes this is one of the finest of all brasses, and is the writer's undoubted favourite. B.L.

THE SUBJECTS

MEN IN ARMOUR

Protective armour of one kind or another, from hardened leather to the modern flak jacket, has always been worn by fighting men. During the centuries when brass memorials were made, armour developed to its peak and became obsolete. The brasses provide us with a marvellous record of the development of armour. Combined with statues in the round, pictures, and pieces of armour which have survived, students of the subject have plenty to work on. In this book I have room for only a brief description of the various developments as they are shown on brasses. Almost every brass varies in some detail or other and, of course, within the dictates of fashion and development every man must have had his preferences. Armour was literally tailored to fit. Long or short legs, thin sticks or shapely calves, big heads, small heads, narrow hips and wide ones all had to be accommodated in inflexible metal with at least a little comfort. Life or death depended upon one's armour and these knights would have had the best they could afford. A man armed *cap-à-pie* must have been an awesome sight as he advanced mounted on a horse which was probably armoured as well. The shining metal and colourful surcoats and mantles, the great helms with the crests making a man look ten feet tall, the clanking, rattling and squeaking noises must have made the knights seem as impregnable as modern tanks.

We tend to think that armour was fearfully heavy, but in fact it weighed fifty or sixty pounds, spread out over the body. Heavy enough, but no more than the modern fully equipped infantryman carries. It may have been difficult to mount a horse unaided, but once unseated, although it must have been extremely dangerous to fall inside that hard metal, it was certainly possible to get up on one's feet again. The fallen knight, unless stunned, was not stranded on his back like an upended tortoise, easy prey for his adversaries.

Armour was also surprisingly flexible, chain mail particularly. Plate armour was articulated where necessary by means of rivets on the top plate passing through a long slot in the lower plate, thus enabling the plates to slip across to a certain extent like the laminations of a lobster's tail. All kinds of cunning hinges and fastenings were invented to increase flexibility. Plate pieces were strapped on rather like cricket pads. Nevertheless movement was restricted, and it must have been a blessed relief to get the stuff off.

Beneath the armour men wore padded felt suits, GAMBESONS or HAQUE-TONS. Many foot soldiers wore these suits without the armour on top, and they did in themselves provide some protection against swords and arrows. It was very necessary to wear something beneath armour, particularly mail. The flexible mail could inflict bad bruising, as it was banged against flesh by weapons, and could even be driven right into the flesh. It must have been most uncomfortable to sit on it on a hard wooden saddle, and it must have chafed terribly everywhere. At the time of the Norman conquest, two hundred years before our earliest brasses, chain mail was commonly worn, and the Bayeux tapestry tells us exact and interesting facts about it. We see men carrying the suits on long poles threaded through them so that they hung and could not kink. It was important that the mail neither kinked, bent nor broke. We also see dead men being stripped of their mail like rabbits being flayed (and they appear to be naked underneath). Mail was very valuable and was an important prize of war. It was only thus that the poor foot soldier could get hold of a few pieces of protective armour.

By the end of the thirteenth century, when we have our first records in brass, mail had changed a lot. It was made by linking rings of steel through each other, rather like coarse knitting. There has been a lot of speculation about types of mail because in some brasses it appears to consist of bands of rings attached to a base, and some authorities have assumed that this so called banded mail was an alternative to the ordinary linked mail. However, it seems that, in fact, there was no such thing as banded mail. Because the engraving of

large areas of brasses had to depict mail, each engraver developed a simplified style by which to represent it, and in some cases this gives the banded effect. It is by comparing these styles that it has been possible to conclude that various brasses were made by the same hand or at least in the same workshop.

The brass of Sir Robert de Septvans shows big areas of mail, and on the right ankle this has been engraved differently from the rest (fig. 17). Some authorities claim that the whole of the mail was intended to be done this way and therefore that the brass was never finished. This seems unlikely. Logically, having completed the first stage of engraving the mail, one would not start again to finish it off right in the middle, but either at the top or the bottom. There are other engraver's mistakes on this brass (fig. 3) and it would seem more likely that this was an attempt to find a better way to depict mail, tried out where it would notice least, which the master engraver didn't approve of, and was therefore not continued with. Or it was quite simply a careless mistake.

The first few great military brasses in this country all show their subjects in mail (figs. 4, 17, 18, 19). Only Sir Robert de Septvans has his COIF DE MAILLES, the balaclava helmet-like head protector, pulled down to show his beautiful curly hair. At that time the coif de mailles was part of the HAUBERK or body covering of mail which hung down below the hips. Later the coif de mailles became a separate item. His mail gauntlets also hang loose; they are part of the hauberk, but have slits in the palms so that the hands could be slipped out. They have wrist straps to keep them in place. The upper legs are protected by padded trews or CUIS-SEAUX. The lower legs are protected by stockings of mail called CHAUSSES. All the knights wear GENOUILLERES or kneecaps, probably made of hard-

18 SIR ROGER DE TRUMPINGTON,
1289

Trumpington, Cambridgeshire

A fine early brass. A chain runs from his belt
or cingulum to the great helm, and at the
apex of the helm is a little staple to take the
heraldic crest or lady's scarf, known in
chivalrous phrase as the "kerchief of
pleasaunce". The shield which bears the
punning arms "azure, crusuly, and two
trumpets in pale, or" is unfinished, as one of
the crosses is in clear relief and the rest of the
shield should also have been cut away to
match, when it would probably have been
enamelled in colour. The ailettes and sword
scabbard are decorated with the arms, but
there is no other decoration whatsoever upon
the surcoat. T.C.

boiled leather or *CUIRIBOUILLI* *(fig. 4)*.
Those of Sir John d'Aubernon and Sir
Robert de Bures are tooled and decorated.
Sir Roger de Trumpington and Sir Robert
de Septvans both wear *AILETTES*,
decorated flaps of leather which stuck up
from the shoulders to protect the neck and
shoulders from side-swiping swords *(fig.
17, 18)*. Although they appear to face forwards in the engravings they were probably set at more of an angle, which would
have been hard to show in two dimensions.
All wear *PRYCK SPURS*. Sir Roger
has his great helm behind his head as a
pillow *(fig. 18)*.

The knights carry big shields, usually
slung on a *GUIGE* or shoulder strap
(which neither of the Sir Roberts has). Sir
John's shield is shown whole, flat, facing
forward. Sir Robert de Septvans has half a
shield and the eye of the viewer supplies the
rest. The other two have carefully drawn
shields showing the curve back round the
left shoulders. Sir John carries a lance with
a pennon tucked inside his right arm and
held at the bottom in the jaws of his lion
footrest. All wear enormous two-edged
swords slung on double belts across the
fronts of their bodies, slightly to the left.

The most characteristic linking factor
is that all four are wearing surcoats. Loose
garments, probably brightly coloured,
and decorated with their armorial bearings
or badges, which helped to identify them
to friend and foe in a throng of armoured
and helmeted men. The surcoats protected
the mail from rain and muck to some extent
– mail was not, of course, of stainless steel!
They are belted with a cord or *CIN-
GULUM* at the waist, and slit right up the
front to be comfortable when riding.

Sir William Fitzralph shows very
clearly the beginnings of the transition to
plate armour *(fig. 19)*. He has half *BAIN-
BERGS* or *GREAVES* on his shins, long
narrow *SABATONS* or *SOLLERTS* on
his feet, articulated to allow flexion of the

19 SIR WILLIAM FITZRALPH, 1323
Pebmarsh, Essex
A splendid military brass in good condition,
except that parts of the dog and shield are
missing. Note the edge of the haqueton
appearing just below the chain hauberk and
the padded cuisses just showing below that.
Both surcoat and shield are fringed. He has
splendidly decorated genouilleres, and the
palettes or roundels at the shoulders, and
coudieres or elbow pieces have sharp points.
T.C.

20 SIR JOHN DE CREKE, 1325
Westley Waterless, Cambridgeshire
Detail of bascinet and aventail. The unusual
fluted bascinet has a little staple at the apex to
take a heraldic crest, or a lady's scarf as a
favour. T.C.

21 SIR JOHN DE COBHAM, 3rd
Baronet. Brass laid 1354
Cobham, Kent
Detail showing studded chausses, probably
with small metal plates behind. Also saucepan
lid genouilleres. T.C.
The inscription, not shown here, reads "The
Founder of the place, once called Cobham, was
made and formed out of the dust of the earth
and into earth and to earth he has again
returned. May the Holy Trinity have mercy
on his soul." T.C.

foot. He has round ailettes to protect his
shoulders, round *GARDESBRAS* to protect his elbow joints. He wears a *HALF
REREBRACE* on his upper arm and a
HALF VAMBRACE on his lower arm.
These two were usually connected behind
the gardesbras. These features continue
with extensions and design differences
right through to the last plate armour made
centuries later.

Sir John d'Aubernon, son of the knight
with the lance, of the same name, and Sir
John de Creke *(figs. 10 and 25)* represent
the next developments. They both wear
the much shorter *CYCLAS* over their
armour. The hauberks dip decoratively
and protectively at the front. The coif de
mailles has been abandoned for the tougher
and more practical *BASCINET*, a plate
metal helmet with rings *(fig. 20)* round its
lower edges – *VERVELLES* – from which
hung the *AVENTAIL*, the mail neck and
chest protector. Both wear tubular vambraces under the sleeves of their hauberks.
Sir John has *ROWEL SPURS*. Both
appear to be wearing jerkins of small steel
plates laced together and riveted to cloth
or leather known as *BRIGANDINE*
work. The lower edges of these show
clearly under the cyclas and over the
hauberk.

About 1340 the cyclas was abandoned
for the *JUPON* which persisted until
1405. There are many fine brasses of this
period and they all show the jupon. This
was a close-fitting leather coat. To begin
with, it had small metal plates riveted
inside it as brigandine work, but by 1380 it
was worn over a plate metal cuirass worn
back and front. This accounts for the wasp-
waisted, bulging chested shape of the
knights of this period. Study the stone
memorial to the Black Prince in Canterbury Cathedral and you will see this
clearly in three dimensions. Gussets of
mail protected the armpits and a mail skirt
or *BRAGUETTE* was worn under the

jupon below the waist. The chausses or thigh guards of the earlier knights of the period, clearly seen on Sir John de Cobham (*fig. 21*), are also brigandine work, the spots representing the rivet heads. About 1375 these too were replaced by plate *CUISSES*. The shoulders of these knights were protected by laminated *EPAULETTES* and the arms and legs fully covered by plate armour. Sir John de Cobham has genouilleres which appear to have handles on them. Pointed knee guards, or *POLEYNS* were sometimes worn and these may be a version of this feature. The bascinet and aventail continue, but the sword has moved right round to the left, slung on a narrow, simple, decorated leather belt or *BAUDRIC*. The *MISERICORD*, a small narrow dagger worn on the right hip, either slung to the lower edge of the braguettes or to the baudric, appears. Its name is supposed to signify that it was used to put fallen enemies out of their misery by being inserted through gaps in their armour. Plate gauntlets with articulated fingers have replaced mail mittens.

After 1410 the jupon also disappeared, and chain mail aventails were replaced by plate throat protectors or *GORGETS*. Rectangular or round *PALETTES* protected the armpits. *BRAYETTES*, skirts of overlapping plates protected the lower half of the body. Peter Halle has simple but perfect armour of this type (*fig. 5*). Sir Simon de Felbrigg (*fig. 72*) has very long epaulettes and big decorated palettes, fine gauntlets, sword, misericord, and the Order of the Garter strapped below his left knee. Sir Richard Attelese (Page 95) and Sir John Peryent (*fig. 12*) wear their baudrics low and square to carry both hand weapons.

By the end of the fifteenth century firearms were being used in battle, and armour was becoming obsolete for war. However it persisted for long for jousting and cere-

22 HENRY PARICE, 1466
Hildersham, Cambridgeshire
A knight in Milanese armour. The elbow guards appear to be held in place by toggles, and there is a lance rest and hook on the right breast of the cuirass. The left shoulder guard is much enlarged. This is tilting armour, designed to protect the vulnerable areas in this game of war. This brass has a fine canopy.

23 THOMAS AND ANNE
NEVINSON, 1590
Eastry, Kent

A nice Elizabethan brass. The Nevinsons died
in the years after the defeat of the Armada.
Thomas was a local military bigwig, being a
Scoutmaster and captain of the light horse of
St. Augustines. As such, he would have been
concerned with the defence of a vital corner
of England in extremely dangerous times
when Spain continually threatened invasion.
This brass is on thin English plate, and has
many small dents and blemishes. The
engraving, which was always shallow, is
wearing very thin in places. The two figures
are half turned towards each other, and Anne
Nevinson seems to have been a small woman
with a burly husband; the pose is most
natural and pleasing. B.L.

24 JONE DE COBHAM, 1298
Cobham, Kent

Although Jone died in 1298 the brass was not
laid until 1320. She was the daughter of Sir
Robert de Septvans of Chartham, and was the
first wife of John de Cobham who died in
1299. This brass is also the earliest one with a
canopy. It has an inscription in separate brass
letters in Lombardic type, each separately
inlaid in the Purbeck marble casement. This
inscription reads: "Dame Jone de Cobham
lies here. May God have mercy on her soul.
Whoever will pray for her soul shall have
forty days' pardon." This inscription in
Norman French gives the brass its description
as a "pardon" brass. T.C.

monial use. Continental armour made in Germany or particularly Milan was all the rage, and it was designed specifically for jousting *(fig. 22)*. The left shoulder where the lance would connect was very strongly reinforced; the elbow guards were curved and fluted to deflect the lance point, with the left side again much bigger. Armour of this period has an unbalanced, exaggerated appearance. Then the skirt got shorter and a pair of plates known as *TASSETS* hung from it by straps to protect the thighs.

Sollerts became ridiculously long and pointed until in 1463 this was forbidden by law; a law more honoured in the breach than the observance until the church was asked to back it up by excommunicating offenders – a severe penalty for being way out. They were replaced by the equally wide *SABATONS*, whose width was in time also regulated by law. Sometimes the knights wore *TABARDS* (second half of the fifteenth century), which were short loose coats with short sleeves bearing their heraldic insignia. The tabard is still a common ceremonial garment. John Shelley (see frontispiece) a typical early Tudor knight, is dressed in this style. Bascinets were a thing of the past and the knights frequently have long hair. Helmets were still worn, the great helm for jousting, and tin hats called *SALLETS* or *SALADES*, close fitting with an extension at the back to protect the back of the neck. The mail skirt hanging behind the tasses reappeared at this time.

From then on, until armour disappeared altogether, it was far more ornamental than practical. It became light, and elegant, chased, engraved and inlaid. It still consisted of the same basic parts but with many laminations to allow for ease of movement. It was usually shaped in the same way as the fashionable clothes of the period. The long pointed *PEASCOD* cuirass being a prime example of this. Thomas Nevinson is wearing typical armour of this style *(fig.*

23). Many of the knights shown on the rectangular plates which then became popular as memorials wear armour of this late period.

Argument over the right terms to use for armour parts rages; the words are mostly Norman French or derived from that language, but what matters is that there is some sort of standardisation of usage. The terms used throughout this book are those which have been accepted by most authorities to be correct by usage. *(See drawings 1, 2, 3, 4 and 5, overleaf)*

CIVILIANS AND WOMEN

For the student of fashion there is so much interesting detail on brasses, and one could spend years making rubbings of, and studying, particular aspects: hair-styles, headgear, shoes, sleeves, embroidery, jewellery and dress-styles in both men and women. Fashions were a lot slower to change than they are today, but change they did, and were just as all-pervasive as they are now. Many of the ladies and gentlemen really did own the fashionable clothes in which they are drawn, but often it was just that the engravers contracted to produce a brass in the style of the times – perhaps with the addition of one or two personal features.

On one occasion I was studying brass rubbings in the print room of the Victoria and Albert Museum. Also working in the room on modern fashion prints were a group of students. We had to unfold and spread out the big rubbings to look at them, and it was not long before the students were totally distracted from their own work, and were exclaiming in delighted interest at the fashions on the rubbings. Only one of them had any idea that brasses even existed, and the notion that they could be relevant to their own work was quite new to them. I have often wondered if any of them followed it up. So many of the women's fashions, especi-

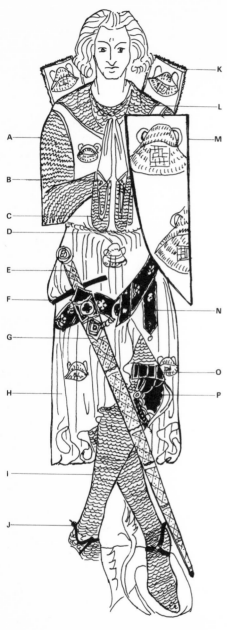

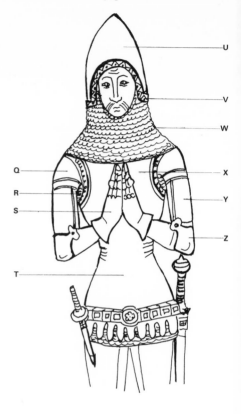

A	HAUBERK
B	HAQUETON OR GAMBESON
C	GAUNTLETS
D	CINGULUM
E	HILT
F	QUILLON
G	SWORD IN SCABBARD
H	SURCOAT OR BLIAUS
I	CHAUSSE
J	PRYK SPUR
K	AILETTE
L	COIF DE-MAILES
M	SHIELD
N	SWORD BELT
O	CUISSE
P	GENOUILLERE
Q	EPAULETTE
R	GUSSET
S	GAUNTLET
T	JUPON WITH BRAGUETTE BENEATH
U	BASCINET
V	VERVELLES
W	AVENTAIL OR HAUSSE-COL
X	JUPON WITH CUIRASSE BENEATH
Y	REREBRACE
Z	COUDES

No. 1   SIR ROBERT DE SEPTVANS
No. 2   SIR RICHARD ATTLESE

A   BANNER
B   GAD
C   GAUNTLET
D   REREBRACE
E   SWORD ARM
F   COUDES OR GARDESBRAS
G   BAUDRIC
H   MISERICORD
I   BRAGUETTE
J   CUISSE
K   POLEYN
L   GREAVES OR BAINBERGS OR JAMBES
M   SOLLERET
N   BASCINET
O   GORGET
P   PALLET
Q   EPAULETTE
R   CUIRASS
S   BRIDLE ARM
T   ARMING POINT
U   VAMBRACE
V   POMMEL
W   HILT
X   BRAYETTES
Y   QUILLON
Z   ROWEL SPURS

Tudor Tabard　　　　　　　　No. 4

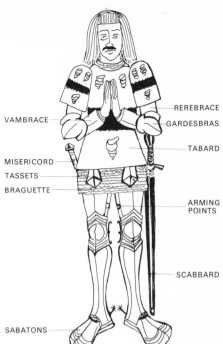

REREBRACE

VAMBRACE

GARDESBRAS

TABARD

MISERICORD

TASSETS

BRAGUETTE

ARMING POINTS

SCABBARD

SABATONS

Plate Armour　　　　　　　　No. 3

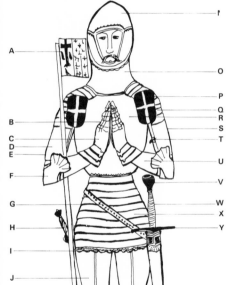

Side View of Bascinet with Visor
Attached, and with Chain Aventail　　No. 5

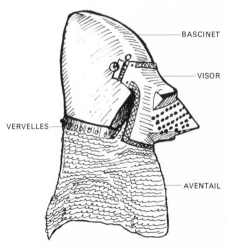

BASCINET

VISOR

VERVELLES

AVENTAIL

No. 3　SIR SIMON DE FELBRIGG
No. 4　SIR JOHN SHELLEY

ally those of the fifteenth century, could be copied exactly in modern materials and be superb. In fact, I am sure dress designers do use brasses as one source of inspiration.

MEN'S AND WOMEN'S FASHIONS

Jone de Cobham wears the typical simple dress of the early fourteenth century. Its loose, graceful folds lent themselves readily to representation by a good engraver, and this particular one was good enough to take advantage of his chance (*fig. 24*). The curve of the right leg shows realistically beneath the *COTE HARDIE*. This garment has short sleeves, and the tight-buttoned sleeves of the *KIRTLE* beneath show clearly.

Lady de Creke's clothes are even more beautifully drawn, the engraver having used what is called the hook technique to represent folds. He has worked out a design which makes her supreme among the female brasses (*fig. 25*). The cote hardie is held up over one arm to show the kirtle beneath, and a *MANTLE* fastened across the breast hangs from her shoulders. Here is a perfect combination of stylisation and realism.

Margaret Torryngton has a cote hardie with long *LIRIPIPES* decorative strips which hang down from the short sleeves (*fig. 26*). Her husband, Richard, also wears a cote hardie, slit right up the front, with a hood attached. Their basic dress is really much the same.

The fine brass of Alianora de Bohun in Westminster Abbey shows the kirtle and mantle worn with *COUVRECHEF* and pleated *GORGET* of the widow. The whole design has classical elegance, but little warmth. She is recognisable as a great lady, but not as a personality.

One of the anonymous brothers at Shottesbrook (*fig. 52*) wears the typical civilian dress of the 1370s; a full calf-length *TUNIC* buttoned on the right

25 SIR JOHN AND LADY DE CREKE, 1325
Westley Waterless, Cambridgeshire
A marvellous brass, realistic and beautifully engraved. The design and engraving of the lady's dress have been superbly handled. T.C.

26 RICHARD AND MARGARET TORRYNGTON, 1356
Gt. Berkhampstead, Hertfordshire
This simple brass has great charm because of its realistic pose and detail. Both wear very similar clothes, and Margaret's right leg swings across to place a restraining foot firmly upon the back of a rather resentful-looking dog, whose overfed companion sleeps peacefully with rounded back, oblivious of Richard's very realistic lion. T.C.

shoulder and thrown gracefully over the left, with a hood attached and a *GIRDLE* on which hangs the *ANELACE* or dagger *(fig. 27)*.

During the fifteenth century the women's dress was a series of variations and developments on the theme of a tight-fitting kirtle worn under a mantle, fastened across the breast with a cord. Elizabeth Halle *(fig. 5)* wears a kirtle with a hip belt under a sideless cote hardie. Margaret de Felbrigg *(fig. 91)* wears a plain, tight-fitting kirtle swelling into full folds below the hips, surely the most feminine and graceful of styles. Elizabeth Felbrigg also favours this style with buttoned sleeves *(fig. 28)*. Another variation modelled by

Lady Peryent and Salman *(figs. 12 and 29)* shows the kirtle cut very full but worn in folds or pleats held tightly at the waist. This, together with a neat double collar and a hedgehog at her feet and topped by a superb and unique head-dress, makes her undoubtedly the best-dressed woman of her time, and she must have upstaged many of her contemporaries with her fine effigy.

Joan Fineux *(fig. 30)* wears the kirtle without a mantle, but she has beautiful bag sleeves to make up for it. Lady de la Pole *(fig. 31)* also left off her mantle, to show the tight-fitting, buttoned kirtle with long, narrow liripipes. Isabella Cely *(fig. 71)* wears the same dress as Joan Fineux. Dress remained substantially the same until Elizabethan times.

The men wore long tunics but by the middle of the century tunics were getting shorter and by the end of the century they were very short. Sleeves were full and gathered at the wrists and these for obvious reasons were known as thief sleeves. By the middle of the century the *GOWN* was coming into fashion and it was worn belted, and edged and faced with fur. Richard Manfeld *(fig. 48)* wears a stylish short gown, and William Pyrry and Richard Westbrooke wear theirs to their ankles. Robert Fairfax early in the sixteenth century has added fur to cuffs and front facings *(figs. 32, 33 and 34)*.

Elizabethan styles of dress for both men and women are almost too familiar to need description, and are faithfully recorded on brass *(figs. 35 and 36)*. Ruffs were worn by both sexes; the women wore petticoats and overgowns, with lots of brocaded and crusted embroidery and farthingales beneath their clothes to distort and distend the hip line *(fig. 14)*. The men wore doublets and trunk hose, but these show more clearly on the military brasses *(fig. 23)* as they also wore full fur-faced gowns and all the civilian brasses

27 WOOLMERCHANT
Northleach, Gloucestershire
Detail showing girdle and anelace.

28a and b ROGER AND ELIZABETH
FELBRIGG, 1380
Felbrigg, Norfolk

Roger de Felbrigg was the son of Simon and Alice Felbrigg. The complete brass has a long inscription which reads "Symond de Felbrigg lies here: God have mercy on his soul. And this effigy is made in remembrance of Alice who was his wife, who lies buried at Harling and not here: God have mercy on her soul. This effigy is made in remembrance of Monsieur Roger de Felbrigg, who died in Prussia, and there his body is buried: God have pity on his soul, Amen, Amen. Lady Elizabeth who was the wife of Monsieur Roger de Felbrig lies here: God have mercy on her soul, Amen." Roger was Lord of the Manor of Felbrigg in 1352, was taken prisoner in the wars in France in 1355, but was later released. He died abroad in about 1380. There is some confusion as to whether the inscription should read "p'ras", Paris, or "prus", Prussia, as the place of his death and burial, but Prussia is probably correct. Roger de Felbrigg is shown wearing a pointed bascinet, aventail, laminated epaulieres, rerebraces and coutes, vambraces, mail hauberk protecting the body and, on this brass visible only at the armpits, breastplate of steel worn over the hauberk and covered by the silk jupon, cuisses, genouillieres, jambarts covering the legs, and pointed sollerets. B.L.

29 SALMAN, 1420
Horley, Surrey
Another very beautiful brass with a fine
canopy. The dress is superb, particularly the
flowing sleeves, and the variation on the
crespine style head-dress is most elegant. T.C.

30 THOMAS BROCKHILL AND HIS
WIFE JOAN FINEUX, 1437
Saltwood, Kent
There is a damaged canopy and inscription
which reads: "Here lies the body of Thomas
Brockhill, gentleman, and . . . his wife, on
whose souls may God have mercy, Amen."
A typical brass of its period, a little stiff, but
redeemed by the nice engraving of the bag
sleeves. Many of the Kent brasses in this
general area show similarities which make
one believe them to have been engraved in
the same workshop. B.L.

32   WILLIAM PYRRY, 1470
Ware, Hertfordshire
Rather an ugly brass, clumsily executed, but
with a certain charm. The two identical
wives indicate that this was a mass produced
brass in which the two female figures were
made from one template. The head-dresses,
collars and cuffs are a little unusual. Space has
been left on the inscription for additional
information as to dates of death which was
never, alas, filled in. T.C.

**31   SIR JOHN AND LADY DE LA
POLE, 1380**
Chrishall, Essex
A fine brass with a good triple·canopy. This
pair resembles the Felbriggs (fig. 28) in pose
and style, and are dated the same. Even the
lions are twins and in each case the man
stands at the woman's right, which is slightly
unusual. Both being East Anglian brasses,
they may have been designed or executed by
the same hand. The de la Pole family became
extremely powerful and wealthy,
intermarried with royalty, and achieved the
Dukedom of Suffolk. T.C.

33   RICHARD WESTBROOKE, 1485
Gt. Berkhampstead, Hertfordshire
A simple brass showing typical civilian dress
of the period. T.C.

34 ROBERT AND AGNES FAIRFAX, 1521
St. Albans, Hertfordshire
A small brass showing slightly more detail than most of its time. Agnes has a dog, and a nice pedimental head-dress. The inscription in English is well cut and easy to read. T.C.

35 WILLIAM YELVERTON AND HIS WIVES, ANNE AND JANE, 1586
Rougham, Norfolk
Surely the effigy of Sir William at least is an attempt at portraiture. He wears a fur-trimmed coat with attached cape, and his two wives, for a change not identically dressed, show very clearly alternative dress styles of the period, their collars and sleeves being totally different. T.C.

36 VINCENT BOYS AND HIS WIFE MARY, 1558
Goodnestone, Kent
The brass is in good condition, and the arms and inscription undamaged. It shows very clearly indeed the Elizabethan fur-lined gown of the man and the French cap and puffed and slashed sleeves of the woman. Both wear small ruffs. There was a space left for the date of Mary's death but it was never filled in. B.L.

37 DAME JONE DE COBHAM, 1320
Cobham, Kent
Detail showing wimple and couvrechef. T.C.

show men wearing these garments which completely cover other clothes from head to foot. This must have simplified matters a lot for the engravers, but from our point of view it is rather a pity.

A few late brasses show civilian men in Carolian collars, cuffs, breeches and jack boots.

WOMEN'S HEAD-DRESS
The different hair-styles and head-dresses are a most interesting aspect of brasses showing women, and here again is a subject for specialisation, because no two are exactly alike, except for those on the mass produced brasses. The earliest figures of women are all very beautiful, and gained so much because the design and

38 LADY DE CREKE, 1325
Westley Waterless, Cambridgeshire
Detail showing wimple and couvrechef. T.C.

engraving techniques were still very free and realistic. Jone de Cobham *(fig. 37)* has a lovely face, framed by a wimple completely covering her throat and chin (a style which indicates that she was a widow), as has Margaret de Freville *(fig. 1)*, Lady de Creke *(fig. 38)* and several others. Jone's hair is covered by a veil or couvrechef, and with slight variations this graceful fashion appears on several early brasses.

In the second half of the fourteenth century the fashion changed and there were several styles. Eleanor de Parys has a veiled head-dress which consisted of two kerchiefs, one bound tightly round the head over the forehead and sides of the face, the second kerchief draped over the top, not unlike a nun's head-dress. *ZIG-ZAG*, *RETICULATED* and *NEBULE* head-dresses were very common and were all much the same. Lady de la Pole shows this style very clearly. The hair hangs below to the shoulders where it is gathered into another little net *(fig. 39)*.

In the early fifteenth century the style changed again. Margaret de Felbrigg wears the *CRESPINE* head-dress in which the hair was gathered into jewelled nets worn high up each side of the face, the head being covered by a veil or couvrechef which hangs gracefully down to the shoulders *(fig. 40)*. Joan Peryent *(fig. 41)* wears a head-dress which is unique and most impressive; one feels that she must have been a leader of fashion who demanded that she be represented as such on her memorial! The crespine head-dress developed until it became almost a caricature. ? Salman has a crespine head-dress with veil which would not disgrace the Royal Enclosure at Ascot *(fig. 42)* and Elizabeth Halle also has a very fine wide arrangement of hair and jewelled veiling on a wire frame *(fig. 43)*. Then the style narrows, and the lady with her head on a pillow illustrates the next development.

39 LADY DE LA POLE, 1380
Chrishall, Essex
Detail showing nebule. T.C.

40 MARGARET DE FELBRIGG, 1416
Felbrigg, Norfolk
Detail showing crespine. B.L.

41 JOAN PERYENT, 1415
Digswell, Hertfordshire
Detail showing unique framed crespine
head-dress. T.C.

42 ? SALMAN, 1420
Horley, Surrey
Detail showing crespine. T.C.

Note the small jewel between the horns *(fig. 44)*. Christina Phelyp has really over-done things with horns as long as her face *(fig. 45)*.

Then the hair was dragged back from the face, and the nets and supporting frame-work moved behind the ears, with the veil of light material falling back away from the shoulders. Brasses showing this style are always in profile, because otherwise it could not have been drawn. There are one or two examples of this butterfly head-dress, Margaret Peyton of Isleham *(fig. 80)* being more attractive than most.

There followed a complete change in the early sixteenth century. The *PEDI-MENTAL* head-dress consisted of a cap over the hair attached to a stiff embroi-dered band which framed the face and met in a point at the top. It is sometimes called the dog kennel style because that is rather what it looks like. The queens in a pack of cards wear pedimental head-dresses. Many brasses show it, none more clearly than that of Elizabeth Shelley *(fig. 46)*. Tudor brasses of the mid sixteenth century often show the dog kennel head-dress with the long flaps pinned up, Thomas Manfeld's two wives both favour this style *(fig. 6)*.

Then for a long time the *PARIS CAP* was fashionable and appears on many brasses *(fig. 35)*. It was a close-fitting cap with a curved border, which came over the ears at the front and had a veil hanging behind. This persisted, with variations, the veil sometimes being pinned up. Many paintings of the time show this head-dress and one always thinks of Mary Queen of Scots (who was a fashionable woman) wearing one. It continued to be worn even under hats, and from now on there are all kinds of variations on the hat theme. They are mostly tall crowned and wide brimmed and would, if worn today, be in the height of fashion. There is nothing new under the sun!

43 ELIZABETH HALLE, 1430
Herne, Kent
Detail showing crespine. B.L.

45 CHRISTINA PHELYP, 1470
Herne, Kent
Detail showing horned. B.L.

44 ANON
Detail showing horned. T.C.

46 ELIZABETH SHELLEY, 1526
Clapham, Sussex
Detail showing pedimental or dog kennel.
B.L.

47

CHILDREN ON BRASSES

There are few children on early brasses, but by the time the art was at its height, it seems to have become the fashion to show all the children of all the wives. Infant and child mortality was terrifyingly high by our standards but accepted in the middle ages. To survive birth itself was quite an achievement; to survive infancy another; but having done so one had a chance because a lot of natural immunity to disease must have been gained if one had not succumbed. However, successive waves of endemic infections from bubonic plague to influenza swept away swathes of the population, and nobody expected anything different. It was easy enough to find more wives and produce more children. Most wives produced babies or miscarried year after year until it killed them, so some of the huge families shown on brasses were not really big at all by their standards. It was a case of survival of the fittest, and a proportion, a percentage did survive, or we should not be here today. A walk round any churchyard will prove that it is only in the present century that we have reduced infant mortality and early death in western civilisations.

Because so many offspring are shown, do not assume that they were all dead when the brass was made. The presence of the whole family including those who survived the subjects of the brasses, was to provide weepers or mourners as we would call them, and this provides rather a nice touch (fig. 47).

Many brasses do specify and commemorate dead children, and a few are specifically dedicated to them, the Manfeld brass being a particularly interesting one (fig. 48). Chrysom brasses showing swaddled infants, seem to me to be particularly tragic (fig. 49).

Children's clothes, as can be seen from the brasses, were merely small editions of those of their seniors. To decide which children lived to adulthood, and which died young is very difficult, but it is obviously safe to assume that those shown as adults did survive the others, and the inscriptions do sometimes specify the dead children (fig. 50).

ECCLESIASTICS

There are many ecclesiastical brasses,

47 ROBERT INGYLTON, 1472
Thornton, Buckinghamshire
Detail. The sons and daughters of three wives are all shown here, a total of ten girls and six boys, all identically dressed except for two of the boys who do not have pouches at their waists, perhaps indicating that they did not survive to manhood. T.C.

49 ANNE CONSANT, 1606
Upper Deal, Kent
The inscription reads: "I who so soon departed this life have soon begun to live, And I who but now was as nothing, have become one of Heaven's company". This is in Latin by her father who was a master at Kings School, Canterbury, and headmaster of Kings School, Rochester. She is "Anne, the daughter and onely child of Thomas Consant . . . and of Lydeth his wife . . . after 13 yeares married". She lived just a few days more than one month. How one wishes that this wanted and loved only child could have survived a little longer. This brass is under the altar, recessed into the wall.

48 RICHARD MANFELD, 1455
Taplow, Buckinghamshire
An unusual brass showing the son and heir, Richard, his sister Isabella, and his brother John. The first two are the children of Robert Manfeld by his first wife, Katheryne, and the last a child by his second wife. A sad memorial to three lost children. Isabella's flowing hair denotes that she died unmarried and small John is in his shroud. T.C.

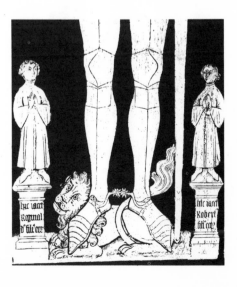

50 SIR REGINALD BRAYBROOKE, 1405
Cobham, Kent
Detail. His two sons, Reginald and Robert, stand on pedestals beside him; both dead as the inscriptions state "here lies". T.C.

51 ARCHBISHOP HARSNETT, 1631
Chigwell, Essex
The inscription (not shown) is sufficient
caption. "Here lies Samuel Harsnett once
vicar of this church, first unworthy Bishop of
Chichester, then more unworthy Bishop of
Norwich, lastly most unworthy Archbishop
of York, who died the 25th day of May,
AD 1631." An extra epitaph reads: "The
reverend Bishop in his great humility
composed the epitaph." He wears cope,
bulbous mitre, rochet and chimere, and
carries a crozier. T.C.

especially of priests in the lower orders.
Bishops and Archbishops and Abbots are
rare, because their brasses were usually laid
in abbeys and cathedrals, and were among
the first to be destroyed at the Reformation. On page 25 is a description of how
Archbishop Harsnett was canny enough to
have his brass laid in a quiet parish church
(*fig. 51*).

Liturgical vestments have remained
unchanged for centuries, so the differences
in the brasses are more those of design and
style than of fashion. The earlier brasses,
like those in other categories, were the
best, the engravers and designers taking
full advantage of the scope given to them
by fine vestments to produce elegant
effigies.

All ecclesiastics are tonsured – they have
a bald patch on top of their heads. A list of
the various garments and terms used will
help to identify and correctly describe
your rubbings of priests.

AMICE, a linen hood usually edged with
embroidery, known as *APPAREL,*
which looks rather like a collar round
the neck.

The *ALB* is a straight robe fastened with a
CINGULUM.

CHASUBLE, a bell-shaped robe with a
hole for the head, and cut away at the
sides. Early chasubles are plain, later
ones have *ORPHREYS* which are H-
shaped pieces of embroidery.

DALMATIC and *TUNICLE,* long-
sleeved gowns with side slits, almost
alike except that dalmatics have more
orphreys.

MANIPLE, a strip of cloth over the left
arm, and *STOLE,* a longer strip worn
across the left shoulder.

MITRE, the familiar peaked hat of the
bishop and archbishop.

INFULAE, the two ribbons hanging
from the back of the mitre.

CROZIER, pastoral staff of the bishop.

CROSS STAFF carried by an archbishop.

53 WILLIAM DE KESTEVENE, 1370
North Mimms, Hertfordshire
William de Kestevene was vicar here from
June 1344 to October 1361, when he died.
This is a unique brass. It is Flemish and must
have been made to order to suit the English
taste with the figure cut out, the polished
marble slab making a background for it. The
figure wears Mass vestments with chalice and
paten. The feet rest on a stag, beneath which
is a bracket supported by two lions
"addorsed". Between the lions is a shield of
arms showing a "saltire cross between four
crosses botanee fitchee". The priest was
definitely identified when documents bearing
these arms and relating to him were found in
Westminster Abbey archives. This is a
bracket brass on which rest the bases of the
side shafts engraved with the figures of the
Apostles in niches. In the centre the figure of
God holds the soul of William, and is flanked
by angels with censers. The side figures are
St. Peter and St. Paul, St. James of
Compostella, John the Evangelist, Andrew
and Bartholomew. In 1859 the brasses were
removed from their slabs and fixed to the
chancel wall. Slabs and burial sites have been
completely lost. T.C.

52 ANON, 1370
Shottesbrooke, Berkshire
Believed to be brothers, as the faces seem to
be carefully drawn portraits, this is a superbly
designed and executed brass. It is an early
brass, and has a beautiful double canopy. The
design and execution of the clothing of the
two men is on a level with that of Lady de
Creke *(fig. 25)*, the hook technique again
being used on the priest's vestments to great
effect. There is a perfect balance between
maniple and anelace, hood and amice. As for
realism, the forehead wrinkles, sagging
cheeks and adam's apples of both men have
been carefully drawn. T.C.

54 ROBERT DE WALDBY,
ARCHBISHOP OF YORK, 1397
Westminster Abbey, London
One of the three surviving brasses of
pre-Reformation Archbishops, distinguished
by the pallium, a circle of lamb's wool with
long pendants back and front, which looks
like the letter "Y" in this rubbing, worn
round the neck, and by the cross staff carried
instead of a crozier. De Waldeby was born in
Yorkshire and became an Austin Friar but
joined the Black Prince on many of his
French expeditions. He was tutor to his son,
later Richard II, Archbishop of Dublin,
Chancellor of Ireland and Bishop of
Chichester before becoming Archbishop of
York. The side shafts of the canopy were
once inlaid with some metal other than brass.
The finial of the arch carries a shield of the
Royal arms of Richard II, the same as those
carried by Simon de Felbrigg *(fig. 72)*. T.C.

55 J. VYNTNER, 1404
Clothall, Hertfordshire
A priest wearing amice, chasuble and maniple
over a cassock. Nicely engraved using the
hook technique. T.C.

PALLIUM circle of white lamb's wool with long pendants worn by archbishops.

CASSOCK, the ordinary dress of the priest usually covered by the other vestments.

SURPLICE, a smaller alb with long hanging sleeves, almost exactly as worn today.

ALMUCE, fur-lined cape with two long ends hanging down in front, worn turned back to show its lining.

COPE, big semi-circular cloak fastened at the throat by a jewelled brooch or *MORSE.*

In many brasses priests carry the *CHALICE* and *HOST.*

ROCHET, long surplice.

CHIMERE, sleeveless coat open at the front *(figs. 52, 53, 54 and 55).*

GRUESOMES, SHROUDS AND SKELETONS

Most of us do not need to be reminded that we are mortal, we are only too aware of it; feeling that our present age is one when destruction and oblivion are only the flick of a switch away. In the days of the brasses, life was desperately short and uncertain, and one would have thought they too needed no reminders at all of death's omniscient presence. Yet there were those conscious enough of mortality to wish to remind others of it by having their own memorials or those to their dead show skeletons, shrouded figures, even worm-eaten ones. These could make an interesting specialist study if you have a morbid cast of mind, but really are not the nicest of brasses.

Many do have great interest, and some poignancy, but unfortunately some are to our modern eyes, really rather comic. The figures in shrouds, with their eyes wide open, look as if they are in some rakish fancy dress costume as boiled puddings. Kathryn Incent has her shroud draped stylishly over her left arm displaying her really enormous feet. So many shroud brasses are like this and seem almost invariably to have been made by very inferior craftsmen. Perhaps the shrouded figure of John on the Manfield brass is an exception *(fig. 43).* He is part of a reasonably good brass and this small figure of a dead child is touching as the clumsy shroud effigies can never be.

ANIMALS ON BRASSES

Almost every knight on the early brasses has an animal beneath his feet, and their ladies usually have a couple of lap dogs. Animals were important heraldically, so naturally many were included on brasses. Heraldic animals always face to the left as you look at them, so they do the same on brasses, as far as the men are concerned. The dogs on the brasses of women are far more relaxed and natural, except that they are so very small and disproportionate. They seem to be no bigger than chihuahuas and this surely cannot have been the case.

The lion was a symbol of courage, so that, used as a footrest, he symbolised the courage of the knight able to subdue lions. The lion was and is a very common heraldic beast and this probably also had a bearing on its constant use. Lions were well known in Europe; after all, the Romans made extensive use of them in their arenas! Yet it is unlikely that the artists and engravers had live models from which to draw, or that they had actually seen full grown lions in the flesh. Even if they had, the practice of stylisation seems to have limited their realism somewhat. The lion at the feet of Sir John D'Aubernon the Younger has enormous paws and claws, very un-lion-like ears, and an expression which could have been the inspiration for the line in the famous limerick about the smile on the face of the tiger (poet's licence to change the species) *(fig. 56).* In fact, the expressions on the animals' faces alone are

56 SIR JOHN D'AUBERNON THE
YOUNGER, 1327
Stoke Dabernon, Surrey
Detail. T.C.

57 THOMAS BULLEN, EARL OF
WILTSHIRE, 1538
Hever, Kent
Detail. B.L.

58 SIR JOHN DE NORTHWOOD,
1330
Minster, Sheppy, Kent
Detail. T.L.

worth a study if you feel light-hearted about brasses; they vary from the smug to the stupid and rarely approach ferocity. Perhaps the engravers used their domestic cats as models, although the only obvious cat I know of is on the helm of Vincent Boys' coat of arms at Goodnestone (*fig. 70*).

Perhaps the most unlikely animal to find is the hedgehog at the feet of Lady Peryent of Digswell (*fig. 12*). The very splendid griffon at the feet of Sir Thomas Bullen of Hever is a most carefully drawn and engraved heraldic fabrication, half bird, half lion, all imagination (*fig. 57*). Sir John Northwood's beast is presumably a lion, but with a square jaw, a chameleon's tongue and shark's teeth (*fig. 58*). There are plenty of fish. A fish was part of the de Septvan's arms and appears on the helms of the stone and brass effigies in Ash by Sandwich church to the members of the same family (*fig. 9*).

There are several elephants, complete with their "castles", the artist's idea of a fortified howdah. The artists can never have seen either elephant or howdah, but nevertheless made recognisable efforts at representing both, even if sometimes the tusks and tails are those of boars, the legs too thin, and jointed like those of horses and other familiar quadrupeds. If you want to find elephants you must visit Wivenhoe in Essex, Cheylemore Park, Withington or Tong in Shropshire.

If brasses are anything to judge by, dogs were as popular as pets and companions then as now. Sir Roger de Trumpington's dog playfully grasping the end of his sword, is superbly realistic (*fig. 59*). A deep chested hound with ferocious feet and a very long feathered tail. A long legged, big dog, suitable companion for his fine master. Sir William Fitzralph's dog is obviously of the same breed, with long flop ears, a short muzzle, and the strong hindquarters of the good runner (*fig. 19*).

In both these animals one sees the characteristics of our present day beagles, bassets and greyhounds, not in those days overdeveloped and specialised as they are now by pedigree breeding, but combined in working, hunting animals.

The long muzzle of the greyhound, looking up at his master is clear on the brass of Sir Thomas de Freville, and on many others *(fig. 60)*. Sir John Leventhorpe's dog is undoubtedly a greyhound *(fig. 68)*.

The ladies owned lapdogs (with fancy collars) and these are shown hiding in their skirts or at their feet, sometimes with their names inscribed. Margaret Torryngton has two unprepossessing little creatures, both of which look bad-tempered and positively overfed *(fig. 61)*. Most of these lap dogs appear to be very small, short-muzzled, lop-eared dogs of indeterminate breed, perhaps like rather long-legged dachshunds. But it is these lap dogs which once again emphasise the continuity of human life and behaviour which makes monumental brasses such appealing memorials. The association between man and his dogs has always been close enough in life to be carried on into death, and in the unselfconscious past it must have seemed logical to include the things you loved in your memorial. The dogs emphasise once again the fact that these brasses are not holy images. The Catholic Church has never allowed animals to have souls to be prayed for, but obviously did not frown upon minor memorials to them.

FOOTRESTS

Mounds and flowers as time passed, the animals were left out and the men and women stood upright upon little mounds of grass and flowers. Sir John Leventhorpe has mound, grass, flowers and dog *(fig. 68)*. In the recumbent stone effigies the feet rest upon the animals' sides, as the

59 SIR ROGER DE TRUMPINGTON, 1289
Trumpington, Cambridgeshire
Detail. T.C.

60 THOMAS DE FREVILLE, 1410
Little Shelford, Cambridgeshire
Detail. T.C.

61 MARGARET TORRYNGTON, 1356
Great Berkhampstead, Hertfordshire
Detail. T.C.

62 NICHOLAS DE AUMBERDENE,
1350
Taplow, Buckinghamshire
This early brass shows Nicholas, who was a
London fishmonger, within the floriated
cross at the foot of which is a swimming
dolphin. T.C.

creatures sit quite normally at the ends of
the tombs. It was the attempt to show in
two dimensions on flat brass the identical
poses of the three dimensional effigies, that
led to the placing of the animal beneath the
feet of the knight, and this rather in-
congruous pose in which the figure was
neither lying nor standing was soon
abandoned for a pose in which the figure
stood naturally upon the grass.

Woolsacks and so on Sometimes the
footrests indicate the trade of the subject
of the brass. The woolmerchant from
Northleach stands upon a woolsack, and
a tailor in the same church is holding a
pair of scissors.

CROSSES, TRINITIES AND ANGELS
There are about twenty brasses of crosses
only, and another twenty which have a
figure on or in the cross. Many more were
destroyed because of the religious significance of the cross *(fig. 62)*.

There are plenty of Trinities on which
God is shown as a rather Germanic looking
bearded man, holding a cross with the
figure of Jesus upon it, and the Holy Spirit
the Dove usually alighting upon the Cross
(figs. 63a, 63b and 64).

Angels appear on several brasses; and
on the stone effigy of Sir John de Septvans
in Ash next Sandwich angels, unfortunately rather mutilated, support his pillow
(fig. 9). Angels, saints and evangelistic
symbols appear on many brasses as
supporting figures *(fig. 52)*.

PALIMPSESTS
The word palimpsest properly describes
a piece of parchment which has been
scraped and used again, but it has come to
mean a brass or piece of brass which has
been used twice. There are many brasses in
this country which have been found to
have engravings on their reverse sides.
This original engraving is almost always

63a and b SIR REGINALD
BRAYBROOKE, 1405
Cobham, Kent

Sir Reginald was the second husband of Lady
Jone de Cobham who was the
granddaughter of the Founder, and only
child and heiress of Sir John de la Pole of
Chrishall. (The Cobham family was
incredibly complicated, but they had one
thing in common – they loved to have
brasses made to themselves.) The single
canopy on Sir Reginald's monument is
surmounted by the Holy Trinity. Notice the
Holy Spirit, the Dove, not sitting on the
cross, but flying, proceeding from the Father
to the Son. On two pedestals at the foot are
represented Reginald and Robert, his sons.
And detail. T.C.

64 JOHN DE COBHAM (THE FOUNDER), 1354
Cobham, Kent
Detail. The Trinity is mounted on a bracket on the finial of the canopy arch. T.C.

65 SIR JOHN NORTHWOOD, 1330
Minster, Sheppy, Kent
This brass has been damaged or altered in the past, and all the lower part is a seventeenth century restoration. A repair job was done in 1881, when this lower half was found to be a palimpsest, the reverse showing the lower portion of a lady with her feet resting on two dogs, probably engraved about the end of the fourteenth century. The armour consists of a globular bascinet laced to the aventail or upper part of the chain mail hauberk. The hauberk has short sleeves and is slit up the sides and middle. The shoulders and elbows are protected by small escalloped plates, probably of cuir bouilli. The gambeson has a scalloped edge showing below the hauberk. At the wrists it has a laminated or feathered pattern, but this may be meant to represent scale work vambraces. Over all he wears the cyclas, long behind and short in front. The shield bearing the Northwood arms hangs on a narrow guige over the right shoulder and rests on the left hip, lower than is usual in English brasses. On the left breast is a rosette-shaped plate with a hook to take the chain for securing the great helm, which is not shown. Sir John's head, unusually for a man, rests upon a cushion. T.C.

Flemish work, which makes it seem likely that there was a very profitable trade between this country and the continent in one-used latten plates. A tremendous amount of sacking of churches went on in the Low Countries at various times, and the brasses were torn up and the bits and pieces shipped over here to be used again.

Palimpsests continually come to light when brasses become loose in their indents and have to be relaid *(fig. 65)*. In many churches you will find small palimpsests mounted on the wall in a hinged frame so that both sides can be studied.

As described on page 13, by the sixteenth century brass was being made in this country, and it was much thinner than the continental laten, so it follows that if you see a late brass on a thick plate it is probably a palimpsest, being a re-used piece of continental laten. In some cases there is no engraving on the reverse, the original design having been filed off and the plate reused. Of course, mistakes were made in engravers' workshops and, rather than waste the metal, it was sometimes turned over and used again. These were known as wasters. Alternatively, the design was altered and adapted. There are cases of whole brasses having been adapted. The most famous of these is at Okeover in Staffordshire, where a whole memorial to William, 5th Baron Zouch of Haringworth in Northamptonshire and his two wives was bodily moved and adapted, altered and re-engraved into a memorial to Humphrey Oker and his wife and children. The second of Lord Zouch's wives becoming a three-tiered picture of the children, with her head turned into a shield of arms. That she was so obliterated has made her much better known than she would have been if left undisturbed!

HERALDRY

Heraldry is a huge subject in itself, and students of it make much use of brasses and

66 SIR SIMON DE FELBRIGG, 1416
Felbrigg, Norfolk
Detail. B.L.

67 THOMAS BULLEN, EARL OF WILTSHIRE, 1538
Hever, Kent
Detail. B.L.

69 SKERNE SHIELD OF ARMS, 1596
Bere Regis, Devon
This plate shows a typical shield of arms, unfortunately defaced by initial scribblers. The crests of castle and tree appear very clearly. T.C.

68 SIR JOHN LEVENTHORPE, 1510
St. Helens, Bishopgate, London
A Tudor brass showing a great helm with a most unusual crest – a man's head. The pauldron guarding the left shoulder is bigger than that on the right side, and Sir John wears a mail gorget or throat protector. The prayer on the inscription has been hacked out. T.C.

70 ARMS OF VINCENT BOYS, 1558
Goodnestone, Kent
Detail. An almost undamaged brass showing a simple shield of arms. The helm carries what appears to be a cat, holding a wreath as a crest. Students of heraldry can decide upon the significance of the bar and crescent on the animal's body.

71 JOHN AND ISABELLA CELY, 1426
Sheldwich, Kent
A reversed photograph of a rubbing of a
typical brass of the period, possibly from the
same workshop as that of Thomas Brockhill
(fig. 30) and Peter Halle *(fig. 5)*, the armour
and dress styles having much in common.
The helm has a striking crest of a hand with
two fingers raised. The knight stands on a
grassy mound with a little plant growing on
it. B.L.

72 SIR SIMON DE FELBRIGG, 1416
Felbrigg, Norfolk
A favourite of Richard II who appointed him
standard bearer on April 7th 1395. His first
wife was Margaret, daughter of Przimislaus,
Duke of Teschen (who was the great-uncle of
Good King Wenceslaus) and his sister Anne
of Bohemia, Richard II's first queen.
Margaret was her cousin and maid of honour.
Sir Simon became the 92nd Knight of the
most Noble Order of the Garter, in place of
Richard Fitzalan, Earl of Arundel, who was
beheaded on 1st September 1397. He took a
back seat after Richard died, through the
reign of Henry IV. For Henry V he was an
active soldier, but did not go to Agincourt.
Sir Simon died on 3rd December 1442 and
was buried with his second wife in Norwich,
in what is now St. Andrews Hall. The banner
is charged with the arms of England paled
with the arms of King Edward the Confessor,
who was one of Richard II's patron saints,
"azure, a cross flory between five martlets
or". B.L.

effigies with armorial bearings in churches to trace lineage and so on. Nowadays, we look on heraldry as being a conceit which has little to do with everyday life. If we accept it as necessary at all it is just for blazer badges or as a highly decorative part of ceremonial. Yet in mediaeval times a man's achievements were often the only way he could be recognised by those who did not know him personally, and even by those who did, when the visor of his helmet was down. One knight looked very like another in full armour, so primary colours, and easily distinguishable symbols were essential if mistakes, both military and social, were to be avoided.

Heraldry began in the early thirteenth century, when the surcoat worn to protect mail was decorated with the wearer's badge, which previously was only to be found on his shield. Hence the term coat of arms which we now use colloquially to cover the whole formal arrangement of devices, although the correct term is *ACHIEVEMENTS*. The next step was to paint the symbol or badge on the front of the helm, and then to make it into a three-dimensional crest which was mounted on the top of the helm. When a knight signed a deed or a paper he did so using his personal seal which showed a figure on horseback with the appropriate symbols on shield and surcoat. Neither he nor his friends could read or write (that was left to the clergy), so the seal was recognisable as his personal signature by its visual symbols. It was natural to pass coats of arms down from father to son, so the complicated art and science of heraldry was born. Only the leaders, the knights, wore coats of arms. Too many would have made battlefields chaotic, for it was the job of the footsoldiers to rally round the banners carrying their leaders' symbols. This is the reason why coats of arms became the prerogative of the aristocrat – the leader. They had in the first place,

nothing whatsoever to do with social snobbery.

The tournament, the war game, where knights wore very complete armour and so would have been completely disguised without identifying badges, also helped to make heraldry important. Originally, many badges were puns, an easy way to convey names to the illiterate. Sir Roger de Trumpington has trumpets on his shields and ailettes *(fig. 18)*.

The heraldic devices were invariably coloured in on the original brasses, but in most cases the enamel or paint has disappeared. Sir John d'Aubernon still has a blue (azure) shield *(fig. 4)*.

Other devices and badges appear on brass. The Order of the Garter worn by Sir Simon de Felbrigg is one of six on brasses of that period *(fig. 66)*. Thomas Bullen, Earl of Wiltshire, father of Anne Boleyn, wears full robes and badge of the Garter and a marvellous collar of red and white Tudor roses, blue velvet garter with gold lettering on his left leg, and white silk scarf over his right shoulder *(fig. 67)*.

Many strange creatures and devices appear as crests on the great helms of the knights which lie behind their heads as pillows. Sir John Leventhorpe has a man's head as his crest *(fig. 68)*. The de Septvans family carry a large fish *(fig. 9)*. The Skerne family coat of arms shows a castle and a tree as crests respectively *(fig. 69)*. Vincent Boys has a cat *(fig. 70)*. John Cely has a pointing hand *(fig. 71)*. Sir Simon is carrying Richard II's banner – he was his standard bearer. It is charged with the Arms of England paled with the arms of Edward the Confessor *(fig. 72)*.

The arms of different families were combined on marriage, and passed down to children, thus rendering the simple original arms extremely complicated, but providing interesting genealogical information. Elizabeth Shelley, born a Michelgrove whose family device was a

73 ROBERT INGYLTON, 1472
Thornton, Berkshire

Robert Ingylton was a barrister, and is shown on this fine brass with his three wives and their respective children. The children are included as weepers. Margaret Dymoke has three sons and five daughters. Clemens Cantilupe has two sons and three daughters. Isabel Lester has one son and two daughters. The inscription reads: "Here lies the pious esquire Robert Ingyltone, Lord of Thornton, advocate in law who died on October 14th 1472. Mary, Queen of Heaven be thou to him propitious, and may Christ the Divine One save hime for the Love of his Mother."
T.C.

74 CHRISTINA PHELYP, 1470
Herne, Kent

Detail. This photograph of the brass shows the fine relief inscription.

63

white falcon, wears a mantle displaying her husband's arms on the left (sinister) side and her own on the right (dexter) side as you look at her. The arms have been impaled. This is the first step in the system.

I can make no attempt here to describe even the basic heraldic terms and their meanings. To enumerate just a few would be of no help at all, as the arms are so complicated and varied that it is impossible to understand and describe them without reference books, unless you have studied heraldry for years.

Coats of arms, shields and so on, on brasses are often very hard to rub satisfactorily. Big areas of the shield may have been cut out and hatched, and this does not rub well. The hatching may have acted as a key to hold coloured enamels. When rubbing shields it is best to work very carefully round the outline first, feeling it with the fingers, and then to pick the symbols or "charges" out one by one and rub them, rather than to rub across the whole surface regardless. The four shields on the brass of Robert Ingylton *(fig. 73)* were difficult to rub and bear no comparison with those on the brass of Henry Parice *(fig. 22)* or the de la Poles *(fig. 31)*.

INSCRIPTIONS

Someone described the inscriptions on brasses as looking like a lot of fencing stakes – in a bad state of repair! And this certainly does apply to some. But you get an eye for inscriptions. They very largely say the same thing so one has an idea of what to expect. One way which I have found useful when an inscription has defeated me for days is to hang it on the wall where I can see it as I work, and try to take nothing but occasional glances at it. Eventually the difficult words become obvious, almost as if the thing were some kind of modern pop art puzzle picture which suddenly comes into focus.

Some of the early inscriptions were in Norman French, on separate letters of brass inlaid in the stone. That of Jone de Cobham is a fine example. The letters are Lombardic capitals *(fig. 24)*. The brass of Sir John de Cobham has a separate inscribed fillet right round it *(fig. 11)*.

By the end of the fourteenth century Latin had superseded Norman French, and Old English or Black Lettering had replaced Lombardic capitals, and Old English language was also being used. The inscriptions were either cut into rectangular plates or occasionally the letters themselves were left in relief and the background chiselled out. This type is difficult to rub well *(figs. 74, 75 and 76)*.

Space saving was important, so the task of reading inscriptions is complicated by the numerous contractions and abbreviations usually noted by the addition of a little line above the nearest vowel to the contraction. For instance, a line over the capital letter "A" indicates "and" and a small "e" over what looks like a "Y" indicates "the". The inscription on the Manfeld brass *(fig. 48)* is a very typical and interesting one, and is fully analysed in J. Franklyn's Book (see Bibliography). The stress marks which look like a figure "2" at the end of each line give the clue that it is meant to be read as a rhyme *(fig. 48)*.

Other inscriptions have gaps in them where a date of death should have been entered, an obvious clue to the fact that the person referred to was still alive when the brass was first laid, and that when they eventually died no one bothered to fill in the details. The Pyrry and Boys' brasses show this clearly *(figs. 32, 36)*.

On other brasses the prayer has been deliberately erased *(fig. 68)*. This was done by Cromwell's men who objected to the link with the Catholic form of worship.

Generally speaking inscriptions became clearer as time went by, and the best part of the very late brass to Mrs. Dorothy Williams who prays beside her own skele-

75 CHRISTINA PHELYP, 1470
Herne, Kent
Detail. It is difficult to rub the letters without picking up some of the backing. Two rubbers are working here – note the masking tape, and the rubbing of the stone in the missing area of the brass clearly showing the old indent lines.

77 DOROTHY WILLIAMS, 1694
Pimperne, Dorset
A late brass, on a rectangular plate. She wrings her hands beside her own skeleton as if she were doubtful of the words she is uttering in a long cartoon-type streamer. T.C.

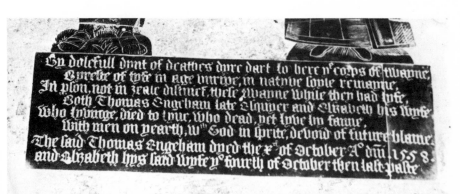

76 THOMAS AND ELIZABETH INGEHAM, 1558
Goodnestone, Kent
The photograph shows a very clear inscription in English of a rhyme which begins: "By dolefull dint of deaths dire

dart . . ." I leave the rest to the reader to puzzle out. It commemorates a husband and wife who died young, within a few days of each other. One wonders what killed them – presumably an infection of some kind which killed them very quickly.

ton, surrounded by a border of skulls, is the clear and simple inscription *(fig. 77)*. It is interesting to note that the conventions of abbreviation mentioned above are both included in this inscription, "Y" with a small "e" above it for "the" and a line over the "O" to indicate the abbreviation of "Anno". In earlier inscriptions the letters are often closed up and spaces omitted as the engraver ran out of space as he approached the edge of the brass plate, but in this case the spacing has been done carefully, with abbreviations and a split word to make it all fit.

Right through the centuries, many people were commemorated solely by inscriptions, and this continues to the present day. There are thousands of old inscriptions. Most of them give the name of the deceased and dates of death, and ask for prayers for their souls, some have verses in Latin or English of much the same type as those which grace tombstones and obituaries right up to the present. Some included personal details; profession and curriculum vitae. Throughout this book, the most interesting inscriptions have been translated where they appear.

As for the language of the inscriptions, Norman French is difficult for most people to translate, Latin is not too bad, with the help of a Latin/English dictionary, and old English can be worked out with a little application, and it helps to be familiar with the works of Chaucer *(fig. 78)*.

78 MARGARITA CHEYNE, 1419
Hever, Kent
Detail. The simple inscription from this brass is a well engraved example of its type in Latin. I leave it to the reader to translate! B.L. The original is of course horizontal.

BRASS RUBBINGS

FIRST STEPS

Of course, it is vitally important that no further damage is done to the brasses we have left. Although there are about eight thousand if one counts all the inscriptions and separate figures, this still represents only a small proportion of the thousands that were made originally. What is remarkable is that even a percentage have survived in reasonable condition, and it does prove that our ancestors were right to choose brass for their memorials. Man has had to tear them up by the roots and rivets to get rid of them. Luckily the older brasses were made of the toughest alloy and, although many bear the scrapes and scratches of nailed footwear, and insecurely fastened bits and pieces have broken off and gone for ever, there is really no reason at all why they should suffer further damage. Constant polishing with metal polishes, all of which contain abrasives or chemicals, wears down brasses very quickly, but the church appreciates this and has put a stop to it, however much eager cleaners would like to see the brasses resplendent and shining. Yet I know of three churches within twenty miles of my home (in one of which no rubbing is allowed for fear of damage), where someone is misguidedly polishing the brasses. Brass rubbing through paper or cloth, carried out with normal materials cannot harm brasses at all, provided they are securely anchored. When brasses are loose in their indents or on walls, then rubbing may damage them, and it is up to the guardians of the brasses to see that they are properly maintained and protected by soft but tough carpeting where they are walked over. To tread upon a bare brass, or even kneel upon it, may damage it, and to touch its surface with any kind of paint, polish, or chemical, except under very special circumstances and with proper permission, is wrong and irresponsible.

These very strong warnings go for the rest of the church as well. The guardians of our churches are set against brass rubbers more by the incidental damage and disturbance they cause than by the damage they do to the brasses themselves. Family parties on a brass rubbing outing, having picnics in the pews, and allowing bored children to have pillow fights with the hassocks, damaging fabric and disturbing worshippers or seekers after peace and quiet, deserve to be kicked out, lock, stock and heelball. Teachers should limit the sizes of parties of schoolchildren or students for the same reasons.

The untidy who leave behind chips of heelball, screwed-up bits of masking tape and the paper their sandwiches were wrapped in, rumpled carpets and switched-on lights, are equally a menace, as are those who rub without first getting permission. The vast majority of brass rubbers behave properly and carefully, but the selfish minority spoil it for everyone.

So take the following steps before you start rubbing and all should be well. First, get permission. If the brass is especially fine, it will be necessary to write to the vicar for an appointment, enclosing a stamped addressed envelope for a reply. The names and addresses of all incumbents can be found in Crockfords Clerical

79 JOHN SEA AND HIS WIVES, 1604
Herne, Kent
A late Elizabethan brass in good condition, although the indent is poor. It has a clear and beautifully engraved inscription. The foreshortening of the photograph makes the already stubby figures look even shorter than they are. The dress of the two women is identical!

Directory, of which every public library has a copy. You may ring him up but if he is a busy man he will be sick to death of such telephone calls and might be a little short with you. Very often the work of supervising rubbers and making appointments has been handed over to a parishoner. Nearly all churches charge for the privilege of rubbing; this can vary considerably, but is usually at least 50p per brass. Small brasses do not command such a fee, and one is usually asked to put something in the church box.

You may take a chance and go along to the church and get permission when you get there. Look in the porch on the notice board and certainly there will be a note stating whether or not rubbing is allowed and where to get permission if it is. Some churches are more organised than others. Blicking in Norfolk where there are several fine brasses, has an appointments book in the church in which all appointments are entered, duplicated forms on which to book a time, a note of the charges, and carte blanche permission to rub if you arrive at a time when no one else has booked (*fig. 79*).

Second, make sure that you are dressed for the job. If the weather is cold, then there is no colder place than an English parish church, for the heating is always turned off except on service days! So take an extra jumper, and a flask of hot coffee. A hand warmer which slips comfortably into the pocket, of the type used by fishermen, can also be very useful.

EQUIPMENT
Be sure that you take enough of everything. It is maddening to find that your roll of paper is just too short to accommodate an exceptionally fine brass. Take plenty of the various types of heelball that you use, plenty of masking tape, a pair of scissors, and a clean duster. Take also a small dustpan and a very soft sweeping brush. Beg

some cardboard tubes from your draper; the type on which dress material is rolled, and use them for carrying and storing paper and finished rubbings. Put strips of Sellotape across one end so that the paper cannot slip through. Shops only throw these tubes away, so will be happy enough to give them to you.

Paper Art shops sell special paper for the job. Architects' detail paper is of good quality and is made of rag rather than wood pulp, and rag paper is best as it does not

80 MARGARET PEYTON, 1484
Isleham, Cambridge
A framed rubbing, gold on black, interesting for her pose with raised hands like Christina Phelyp (*fig. 13*), her butterfly head-dress and her beautiful Venetian brocade dress. The brocade pattern is consistent throughout and the impression of folds is achieved by scored lines. This brass is a fine piece of design which could be entirely modern in its conception.

yellow with exposure. It can be bought in rolls 30, 40 and 60 inches wide and up to 25 yards long and is listed at 70 gr. per sq. metre. Only specialist shops stock the wide sizes. Non-rag white paper in the same categories is neither so tough nor so long lasting and yellows easily. It is a bit cheaper, but it is a bit silly to spend time and money making rubbings on poor quality paper. Prices for paper are not quoted as they are not static. Black Matt paper for gold and silver rubbings is made in 80 gr. and 70 gr. weights, and is a little more expensive. Although the quality is good I do not find the colour or texture very pleasing. I use a very dense black wallpaper with coloured heelball to far more effect; for the velvety blackness shows off the wax properly. Unfortunately the narrowness of wallpaper limits one to single width brasses. Metallic gold and silver papers are made specially for brass rubbing, but again I do not find them very pleasing and plain gold or silver wallpapers can be bought which you may prefer.

Brass rubbing book linen in rolls 40 inches by 7 inches long, in white, black, dark blue, light blue, green and red, is available but expensive. This material makes an excellent durable surface for rubbings which do not need to be mounted, but it is only really satisfactory when used on extremely well defined brasses. The thickness of the cloth makes it difficult to rub finely engraved or very worn lines successfully.

I have used most successfully a thin white cloth containing dressing to stiffen it which is supplied for architects. There is no reason why you should not try various cloths and papers for different effects, but all must be fairly stiff to resist the pressure of rubbing, otherwise they will stretch and move as you work and it will not be possible to do a clear and clean job. Fifty micron aluminium foil suitable for taking rubbings can be bought direct from the

Aluminium Federation, 60 Calthorpe Road, Five Ways, Birmingham 15. Fibre glass resin can be bought locally from some garages and do-it-yourself shops.

Masking tape　Never use clear tape as it sticks to stone and plaster and lifts it, and also sticks too well to brass rubbing paper and tears layers off it. Use masking tape which can be bought in big rolls from any stationers. Three-quarter inch is plenty wide enough.

Heelball　The wax crayon developed from cobblers heelball, which is the most commonly used rubbing crayon. It comes in big sticks or cakes, and in various grades of hardness or softness, and in shades ranging from grey to black. Although most is labelled black, some is blacker than others and is usually preferable. It also comes in colours; a kind of coppery brown, brick red, bronze, gold, and silver and white *(fig. 80)*.

The two best known makes are Astral and Summit wax. Summit wax is softer, blacker and easier for the beginner to use, but in warm weather may be too soft and crumbly and this can spoil the work if you are not careful. Both makes are excellent, and it is really a matter of personal preference. For finishing off work at home, use big and small black Acorn crayons. These are soft and not suitable for rubbing in situ. A crayon pencil which can be sharpened to a fine point can also be very useful for touching up very fine detail.

Erasers　Plastic erasers will remove heelball, but it is extremely difficult to get heavy marks off white paper, and only small light blemishes can be totally erased. Plastic rubbers will get all the heelball off book linen and metallic paper without leaving marks. Really bad blemishes can be removed from book linen with a typewriter rubber used gently.

Spray adhesive　This adhesive in an aerosol is absolutely invaluable for mounting rubbings. It is extremely difficult to mount any but the smallest rubbings perfectly without wrinkles and air bubbles, when using traditional adhesives of any type. Unfortunately these aerosols cannot be sent through the post, so are only available to personal shoppers. Perhaps you can persuade your local art shop to get a supply. They are quite expensive but last a long time.

Lettering　You may wish to title your rubbings. Blick transfer lettering, sold at all art shops, stationers and bookshops, is excellent for this job. Many different types are sold and you can choose the one you like on the spot. Old English or Black Letter looks very well as it matches up to some extent with the inscriptions.

All the specialist brass rubbing materials and the Aerosol adhesive are available from Messrs Phillips & Page, 50 Kensington Church Street, London W8 DA. Most art shops stock some paper and heelball. More about mounting materials may be found on page 81.

BASIC BRASS RUBBING TECHNIQUES

If you live in a parish which has a church containing a brass you will probably have known since childhood something about brass rubbing, if only from having watched others. Many schools take parties of children brass rubbing; but often the first introduction one has is to see a rubbing on someone else's wall and to be attracted to it, and to ask what it is and where it came from. The next step is to find someone to take you along and show you how it is done, but failing such help it is nice to know just how to start. The first thing is to find out where the brasses are. This book, and most books on brasses contains lists noting the better brasses, but there are so many that it isn't possible here to detail them all without taking up far too much space *(see page 87)*. Don't, to begin with, choose one of the huge and splendid brasses. You will have to pay a lot to rub it and it isn't worth spending the money until you have some experience. Find a small, clear-cut brass, get permission to rub and arrive on time for your appointment. If there is a pamphlet about the church it will be in the book rack and it will certainly describe the position of the brass, and they can be very difficult to find; hidden under carpets and pews, behind the organ, or in the vestry, often in cramped, dark corners (*fig. 49*). Switch on only as many lights as are strictly necessary to see what you are doing. Brush and dust the brass carefully to remove any dirt or grit on the surface or in the engraved lines (*fig. 81*).

Then have a really good look at the brass. Use a note-book if necessary and make a rough sketch of it noting where any odd or protruding bits of engraving are, because once the paper is down over the brass it can be very hard to remember and you may find on taking up the rubbing that some vital part has been left unrubbed. Look carefully for protruding rivets, and if they are proud and sharp put a small piece of masking tape over each to prevent it cutting the paper as you hit it with the heel-ball. It is very easy indeed to rub into a rivet and make a jagged tear which can spoil an otherwise perfect job. Tears can be repaired later by backing with Sellotape. Loose or damaged areas of brass should also be noted so that you can be extra careful when rubbing (*fig. 82*).

The figures always lie with their feet towards the altar, so that if they suddenly sit up, as presumably on resurrection day they may, they will come face to face with God.

Decide on the type and size of paper you need, and on just how much of the brass you intend to rub. There is nothing which says that you must rub every little bit of every monument every time. Extremely damaged canopies or inscriptions may be interesting to the specialist but will not look particularly attractive, or may make the rubbing much too big when mounted and hung.

Cut the paper carefully, allowing big margins top and bottom. Excess paper can always be cut off later on but cannot be added, and nothing looks worse than a rubbing running too near the edges of the paper. A foot clearance each end is about right.

Lay the paper carefully over the brass, as squarely as possible, so that the parts to be rubbed are more or less central. Tear off pieces of masking tape about two inches long and stick the edges of the paper down to the stone floor or use longer pieces along the edges of the paper (*fig. 75*). If the brass is on a wall, plaster and colour wash may be marked and lifted by masking tape, so do not use more than is strictly necessary. Having made sure that the paper is well anchored – three or four pieces of tape on each side should be enough on a medium-sized brass – you are ready to begin. Find a hassock to kneel on (replace

81 PREPARING THE BRASS
Before you start rubbing, dust the brass to remove any dirt or grit on the surface or in the engraved lines.

82 PETER AND ELIZABETH HALLE,
1430
Herne, Kent
This photograph of a brass shown in *fig. 5*
rubbed black on white shows quite clearly
what to look for before starting: the damaged
and crumbling casement which can tear and
crease the paper; certain edges of the brass are
flush with the stone, others raised above it;
the missing parts of the sword; the rivet
protruding just below his left knee; the two
ribbon inscriptions and the shield which
could easily be missed altogether; the
delicately cut spurs. (Photograph taken with a
35mm wide angle lens.)

it when you have finished work) place your
box of heelball on the floor beside you, and
have the clean duster to hand. Never kneel
on the paper or on the brass itself. If you
kneel on the paper it will bear forever the
imprint of the floor below, and the movement of your body as you work will shift
the paper so that the rubbing becomes
muzzy. Your hands should, of course, be
absolutely clean at this stage, so wipe them
off. Then, using your fingers, feel for the
edges of the brass through the paper and
follow them round, thus creasing the
paper very slightly against the edge so that
you have an outline within which to work
(*fig. 83*). Take a piece of heelball firmly in
your hand between finger and thumb with
the butt end resting against the ball of the
thumb and, using the flat end of it, not the
sharp edge, begin to rub a couple of inches
in from the edge of the brass. Press firmly
but not too hard to begin with, and work
the heelball backwards and forwards with

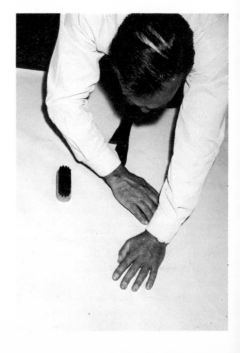

83 MARKING THE EDGE
Pressing the edge of the brass against the
paper; the faint ridge can just be seen above
the rubber's left wrist, down to the righthand
lower corner of the picture.

short strokes overlapping each other, holding the paper steady in the working area with the other hand. Go on until the surface is covered. Try not to leave separate lines which show where every stroke has been made, and work in all directions, up, down and across, in order to blend the strokes together. Strokes made all in the same direction across the brass will show in the finished work like the weave on a piece of material. As your hand warms the heelball, it becomes easier to work with, and in cold weather it pays to keep turning it in your hand and working with alternate ends to take advantage of this. The hardest part is not to go over the edges of the brass and mark the paper, so as you approach the edge slow down and take care, feeling your way (fig. 84).

Mistakes are hard to erase and, although the rubbing can be cut out and mounted and the mistakes got rid of this way, the best rubbings are always unblemished and complete on their original paper or cloth. Very small mistakes and rough edges can always be touched up later but try to do as good a job as possible first time. There is nothing more irritating, and we all do it at times, than working for an hour and not making a single mistake, and then when the rubbing is nearly finished and you are getting tired anyway, going right over the edge and spoiling the appearance of the whole job (fig. 85).

By this time you should be beginning to see the figures coming up under your hands, and your mind, as your hands work, will be thinking about the brass, for your nose will be very near to it, and here I shall digress and point out one or two facts which will become very evident to you anyway. Brass rubbing is very tiring. To hold a kneeling position with the body horizontal, working with one hand and using the other to steady the paper and to support your body at the same time, without bearing down on the paper, is difficult.

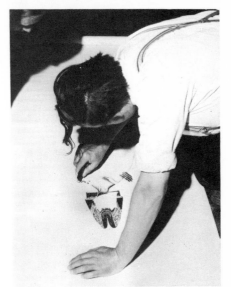

84 GOOD RUBBER FEELING HIS WAY
Working carefully along the edge, having first finger-pressed round the brass. He is not kneeling on the paper, so is forced to rest his weight on his left hand and assume a head-down position, which is very tiring to maintain.

85 RUBBING A VERY BIG BRASS
To rub the very big brass of Sir Simon de Felbrigg and his wife under their canopy, this rubber has removed his shoes so as not to cause damage. He is rolling back the paper as he works downwards, and is forced to kneel on a cloth on the brass itself, as the sides of the pews make it impossible to work from the side of the brass. He has the Victoria and Albert Museum catalogue open beside him so that he can check what he is doing as he works.

86 KEEPING THE COLOUR EVEN
Take care not to over-rub in any one place –
not only will it blur the edges of the white
lines, but it will cause considerable
paper-stretch.

87 FINISHING TOUCHES
Putting the finishing touches to a fine
rubbing of a fine Elizabethan brass. This
rubber has succeeded in getting a very black
impression, and will have only a few minor
blemishes to touch in later. She has made no
mistakes at all.

So sit back on your heels frequently and
consider for a bit. It gives the body a rest
and the brain time to work out the next
step. Some rubbers find they get a headache
and recommend taking aspirin to counter-
act it. Really the answer is to get yourself
in training by only tackling small brasses
to begin with, and by never rubbing for too
long at a time. Get up and wander round the
church for a bit, or sit quietly in a pew; there is much else to look at. Or go out into
the churchyard with your flask of coffee
and have a quiet cuppa. Very often someone comes into the church, another rubber,
a visitor, the vicar or someone to do the
flowers. Pass the time of day and if it is
someone who knows about the church,
find out all you can about it; but don't
forget that someone else may be waiting
to rub, and you must not waste too much
time chatting. If there are several brasses in
the church, several rubbers may be at work,
and there is often a murmur of quiet talk
and comment, or someone gets up and
comes over to see what kind of a fist you are
making of the job. I learned a lot by studying the techniques of others this way, and I
saw beautiful work which gave me high
standards at which to aim.

Back to the rubbing. By now you should
have a sizeable area done (fig. 86). Keep the
colour even, and don't over-rub in any
one place, particularly over fine or complicated engraving, or the paper may stretch;
in any case too much pressure or constant
backtracking blurs the edges of the white
lines. On engraved decorative areas press
a little harder and try to achieve the blackness you want without too much backtracking. On unengraved areas you can fill
in just as if you were working with crayon
on paper on a table, and backtrack as often
as you like for there will not be little fine
lines to blur.

Don't be disappointed if your rubbing
does not seem to be as black or as perfect as
you had hoped. The blemishes of the

centuries – scratches, pits and dents – will be faithfully reproduced and may give the rubbing a disappointingly bitty look. This can be dealt with later. What is important is that you do get every detail, every outline correctly rubbed without leaving anything out or adding anything. Men usually find it easier to get really dark rubbings as their hands are strong and they press very hard. It is surprising what pressure from the heelball the paper will stand without tearing, but the hard presser does risk a tear if he comes up against sharp edges or protruding screws or rivets. Women generally do not rub so hard or with such sweeping strokes, but take great care and get very good results. It is possible to get a very black impression indeed, but the white lines get thinner each time the paper is rubbed as it moves fractionally across the edges of the engraved lines *(fig. 87)*.

As you work, little bits of heelball will crumble off the stick and accumulate on the paper and these must be removed constantly, but never by brushing them with the back of the hand. The flesh picks them up and carries them across the paper, drawing little faint lines as it goes. Careful flicking with a soft duster or handkerchief is the best way, and always brush the specks outwards and away from you.

Having made sure that you have got an impression of everything that is there, remove the pieces of masking tape and put them in your pocket, not on the floor of the church. Roll the paper back carefully from one end *(fig. 88)*, checking that all the brass has been rubbed; if it has not, replace the paper and tape it down again and do the missing parts. If all is well as you roll back, lift up the rubbing, letting it unroll again, and shake it gently so that all loose flecks of wax fall off, then re-roll it and put it in a tube. Be sure you leave the church as tidy, or perhaps tidier than you found it, turn out all the lights and don't forget to leave some money in the box if you have not paid already. Lock up, return any keys and take your work home to finish it off. There are those who say that no finishing should be necessary, but it is a very good and experienced rubber indeed who can achieve perfection on the spot.

USING COLOURED HEELBALL ON HEAVY PAPER AND CLOTH

There is no basic difference in technique, but if the material is thick it is difficult to feel the brass under the paper with your fingers, and consequently much easier to go over the edges. By the same token the finer and shallower lines do not come up

88 REMOVING THE RUBBING
Make sure you have completed the rubbing before removing the masking tape. Then roll the paper back very slowly from one end checking, as you do, that you have missed nothing. If you have, replace the paper, tape it down again and fill in the missing parts.

75

well, so never use heavy paper or cloth on a shallow engraving.

Gold and silver look well on coloured cloth. Gold does give an impression of something like brass and because the gold wax is lighter than the cloth the rubbing is positive – light with dark lines – rather than negative as are the black and white rubbings. Faces and features look much more alive in positive than they do in negative.

Both gold and silver heelball are a little harder than other waxes and more pressure is needed, as well as very even rubbing technique to prevent streaking. Coloured heelballs are as soft as black. Experimentation with coloured waxes will teach you which colours look well on which papers. The bright chocolate brown wax makes pleasing rubbings on gold, and white wax is effective if rather ghostly, on black. Different sections of a brass may be rubbed in different colours, and this is quite fun. A coloured shield, banner, surcoat, tabards, dress mantle or vestment highlights a black and white rubbing, but do keep the colours heraldically correct as far as you are able to.

REVERSE RUBBING

This is a complicated process and takes a lot of time and care. It can be used on a part of a rubbing such as a shield which you wish to colour. First, make a rubbing with white wax on white paper. This in itself is difficult as it is hard to tell exactly where you have and have not rubbed. At home, draw in with black ink and a fine pen the outlines of the shapes. Use waterproof ink and do the job carefully. Next, take a rag soaked in paraffin or lighter fuel (be very careful not to work with a naked flame in the room or to light a cigarette) and wipe of the wax with it. Refold and redip the rag constantly so that you are working always with a clean face. This will take off the heelball. Squint along the rubbing

sideways to check that all the wax has gone. Leave the paper to dry out thoroughly and then colour in the inked outlines with waterproof (for bright, hard colours) poster paints (for opaque, matt colours) or ordinary crayons (for coloured, wax effect). If the paints will not take, then the surface of the paper is still waxy. A coat of ox gall will help to shift this.

DABBING

To take impressions of indents and for record purposes rather than for decoration, dabbings are very useful, but they take a long time, are not very dark, and are fragile to handle. Make a dabbing pad by wrapping a lump of cotton wool tightly in a piece of chamois leather. Mix powdered graphite (which, if you cannot buy it, can be made by grinding down artists' graphite crayons) with linseed oil to a stiff paste. Use tissue papers. Set the paper up over the brass in the normal way, but press it gently into the engraved lines and round the edges with the finger. Dip the pad into the graphite paste and dab it over all the parts you wish to reproduce. Press the pad down firmly, and lift it straight off without moving it sideways at all. Using such thin paper one gets an accurate impression, so it can be used for study as it really does show up detail which even the eye cannot always pick up on the brasses themselves.

ALUMINIUM FOIL

Rubbings made on foil are quite fun, but they look a little brash and tinny, and it is difficult to get a really fine detailed rubbing (*fig. 89*). The foil is laid over the brass just as is paper, but great care should be taken not to scratch the surface of the brass. No damage at all need be done if the operator is careful. Having taped down the foil, take a soft cotton pad (a handkerchief will do), and rub the brass, pressing the foil down into all the engraved areas. You need to rub quite hard. This is extremely quick to do, and the largest brasses can be rubbed in a fraction of the time it takes to do them with heelball. However, now comes the problem. The foil must not be rolled or have any kind of pressure put on it once the rubbing has been made, so it is quite a job to get it home. For this reason it is best to stick to small or single brasses. See page for details of the finishing process.

FINISHING ALL TYPES OF RUBBINGS

There are those who feel that no rubbing should be touched once it has been taken from the brass. Of course, if your purpose is purely to make a record for a study, then no finishing will be needed as every detail should be there. However, if your rubbing is to be used decoratively, then it will have to be properly finished at home. It very much depends on your own taste and ability exactly how perfect you make the finished job. As a brass lies on the floor of a church one sees it as a whole, all of a colour, and because it is not usually very brightly lit, nor is it polished, many of the small blemishes, pits and scratches on its surface

are not apparent to the eye. On the other hand, your rubbing shows up these blemishes far too prominently, as white, uneven spots and splodges spoiling clean lines, distorting features and obscuring edges. When the memorial was first made, it bore none of those blemishes. A new brass must have been a very splendid thing, often with parts of it coloured in. I am sure that the owners of the brasses would not have accepted badly finished, scratched or pitted work, and I see no reason why rubbings should not reproduce as far as possible the original intention of the engraver and discard the superficial and extraneous damage of the centuries.

It is rather different where parts of the brass are missing. Where there is no real clue as to what has gone, then it is not possible to draw in the missing parts. Often the indent in the matrix will give you some idea, and there is no reason why you should not outline missing parts, such as spurs, sword scabbard or pommels. This balances the picture as it was balanced when new.

You may prefer the rubbings you make to be dark grey, but the blacker they are the more dramatic, and this can be done much more effectively and safely by careful finishing than by over-rubbing the brass on the spot.

For all finishing work, lay the rubbing on a flat surface. I find that my wooden dining-room table is excellent. It has of itself some grain which gives texture to the finished work. If you use a formica table top for finishing the smoothness of the surface produces flat, shiny, finished work (fig. 90). I use the big black Acorn crayons for finishing, small black children's crayons for tricky corners and black crayon pencils for fine lines. The crayon is softer and more crumbly than heelball so take care to flick away loose pieces with a cloth as soon as they appear. Start at the top of the brass and work downwards towards yourself, so that you will

89 MAKING A RUBBING ON ALUMINIUM FOIL
Note the boxwood modelling tool for deepening lines, strips of masking tape and the left hand steadying the rubbing area.

90 FINISHING A RUBBING
Note the different kinds and size of crayon
being used, and the eraser. The blemishes,
such as the rivet in the palm of the right
hand, show very clearly. The cross-hatching
and decoration on the head-dress and the
inscription have not been touched up, but
rubbed firmly in the first place. B.L.

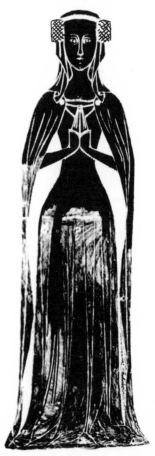

**91 LADY MARGARET FELBRIGG,
1416**
Felbrigg, Norfolk
Margaret was a cousin and maid of honour
to Anne of Bohemia, first wife of Richard II,
to whom Sir Simon Felbrigg her husband
was standard bearer. She was the daughter of
Przimislaus, Duke of Teschen, so was also
cousin of his great-nephew, Good King
Wenceslaus. This rubbing was done in rather
a hurry and when photographed was in the
process of being finished at home. Note the
ineradicable mark where a careless rubber
went off the brass between skirt and mantle
at the bottom righthand side (her left). B.L.

not be leaning over or touching the finished work, which can be allowed to roll lightly as you complete it and move the paper up the table. Outline and tidy up bad edges first with the pencil, then block in big plain areas, with the big crayon and then the small one when the work becomes fiddly. Don't make a completely matt black surface, leave some texture, but take out the scars of scratches and tidy up rivet marks and plate joins so that they are not obtrusive.

Intricate decoration, mail and so on should have been rubbed hard enough on the spot not to need blacking in at all, but big white blemishes should be touched in with the small crayon or pencil.

When the work has been done to your satisfaction, and it may take at least as long as the original rubbing, flick off all the loose wax, and polish the rubbing lightly with a soft clean duster, just enough to smooth the surface and bring up a little shine.

Don't try to get out any mistakes you have made on the figures themselves with an eraser – you will just make a horrible mess. The only way to get rid of black areas, and it is not totally satisfactory, is to touch them out with white poster paint or white ink, or sometimes it is possible to cut out a small matching patch of white paper and stick it carefully over the mistake (*fig. 91*). Where the heelball has got on to the surrounding white paper, then, if the marks are not too dark, they may come off at least partially with an eraser. You have to rub hard and at the same time be careful not to rub right through the paper or to crinkle it.

Touch up gold and silver rubbings exactly as above using heelball. It is difficult to buy gold or silver wax crayons, but gold and silver wooden pencils are obtainable and are extremely useful for touching up. The trouble is that it takes hours to go over a big area with the very thin pencil.

Another time-consuming method, which does turn a gold rubbing into a splendid reproduction of the original brass as it might have been when polished, is to touch it in with an artist's paint brush on the fine parts and your finger on the big areas, using modern wax based gilts. Goldfinger green gold which comes in tubes is excellent for this job. The wax, spread evenly with the finger, dries at once. When using the brush, have a little turpentine handy in which to moisten it before dipping it into the gold, which makes it possible to brush on the gilt. Leave mail or intricate areas of engraving, decorations, embroidery and so on untouched in, and work mainly on the big flat areas of brass; this gives texture to the finished rubbing. Silver rubbings can also be finished in exactly the same way. Leave the rubbing for an hour to two to dry right out and then polish it with a soft duster.

If you are finishing a foil rubbing, lay it face down on a smooth table. Provide yourself with several odd pieces of foam rubber. They can only be used once, so don't use anything too expensive. Fibre glass resin is made by mixing very small amounts of catalyst with the liquid resin, in a jam jar. The supplier of the resin will tell you the exact amount to use. Once the catalyst has been added, the resin begins to set, and will after ten minutes or so according to the temperature of the room in which you are working, become unworkable. The warmer the room, the sooner this happens. Half a pound jam jar full is plenty for one single large figure, so don't mix too much at a time, as you can always make up some more. If you wish to make an extremely rigid figure which will not need mounting, use fibre glass mat as well, as described below, but the resin by itself is sufficient to stiffen the rubbing and fix the lines permanently. Working quickly, using the foam rubber as a swab, put a liberal layer of resin all over the wrong side of the rubbing. Foil rubbings are best cut out when they are finished, so there is no need to go beyond the edges of the figures. Make sure that you have swabbed plenty of resin into all the crevices. This is a messy job and your hands will be covered in the stuff. Do-it-yourself shops which sell resin usually sell special cream or cleaning agents with which to remove it from your hands. Do this while the resin is setting on the back of the foil. Keep a check on how the setting is going and as soon as the rubbing can be turned over without the resin running or sticking to the table, before it has completely set, put it face up, and immediately, using a box-wood modelling tool with a fine round point, run down the main lines of the engraving to deepen and strengthen them. If you work fast, you should get all the lines on a single figure treated in this way before the resin sets really hard. Keep lifting up the foil as you work, so that it does not stick to the table surface.

Leave the rubbing for at least an hour and then, using fine steel wool, go all over its surface. This takes off the tinny look and dulls the shine a little giving a far better finish than the very brash foil. Next, you must colour in the lines of the engraving. One way is to paint all over the surface with black boot polish, wiping off the surplus so that only the indented lines are left dark. I have not found this very satisfactory, as too much tends to be wiped out of the shallow parts. Black Polymer artist's paint, very slightly diluted, can be painted into the lines with a water colour brush. Coloured paint used sparingly on decorated areas – sword belts, shields, girdles, brooches – improves the look of the job. Finally, the rubbing must be cut out with an old pair of scissors, which still need to be pretty sharp, and it is then ready for mounting.

If you wish to back the foil more solidly with fibre glass mat, swab a thin layer of resin over the foil as above, then put a layer of mat right over the surface. Using more resin, swab the mat without pressing it hard, until it goes transparent and blends into the resin. Continue as above until you reach the point where you have turned the rubbing over and indented the lines, by which time the first layer will be set fairly hard. Reverse the rubbing again and put on another layer of resin, and another layer of mat as before. Allow the whole thing to set very hard before attempting to cut it out. The harder it is set, the more brittle it will be and so easier to cut. Smooth rough edges with glass or fine emery paper before painting in the finishing lines.

DISPLAYING RUBBINGS

What to do with finished rubbings is the perpetual problem. One is in the same boat as the keen photographer. There is a limit to the number of pictures or rubbings which can be displayed in your house at any given time, and only a few other aficionados are interested in your work anyway. Yet one or two good rubbings well displayed catch everyone's eye and enhance almost any decor, traditional or modern. The smaller brasses are not on the whole so striking as the bigger ones, but the bigger ones are so hard to find wall space for. To be seen at their best, it must be possible for the viewer to stand well back from them.

The ideal place for display is a hall a landing or a stairway where lighting can be focused on the rubbing and where one gets first a long view, and then walks towards it to consider detail.

An alcove with one wall papered with an unframed rubbing makes an effective feature. Draught screens are out of fashion these days, but are sometimes used instead of room dividers. A three or four panel hinged screen of hardboard, covered with rubbings on bookbinders cloth can look magnificent. Smaller screens or fire screens to hide an empty fireplace could also be made by panelling a rubbing behind plate glass.

From small occasional to very large everyday, tables look well with a black on white rubbing beneath plate glass held in clips round the table edge.

A simple way to display rubbings is to hang them unframed. Use quarter or half inch dowelling. Cut two pieces, one the exact width of the paper for the bottom, and the other one inch longer for the top. Quarter of an inch in from each end of the longer dowel bore a hole big enough to take white nylon blind cord. Thread enough cord through to hang the rubbing and knot it off below the hole at one end. Make fancy knots and tassels if you wish. Then, having cut the rubbing exactly to the length required plus about two inches, turn an inch over to the blank side top and bottom and stick it down with Sellotape, making a hem through which to slip the dowels. Put the dowel with the cord in the top, and thread the cord through the other hole and knot it off. Slip the bottom dowel in the lower hem to make the rubbing hang straight. Should more weight be needed, slip some small lead curtain weights into the hem behind the bottom dowel.

The rubbing can, of course, be stuck permanently to the dowels, but the method described allows the same hangers to be reused for another rubbing when you feel like a change.

Even simpler, use black or white plastic poster hangers. These are triangular in section, open at the apex. Slide the strips carefully along top and bottom edges of the rubbing. If the paper is too thin and will not hold in the plastic strip, fold it over once before putting the strips on. Rubbings hung this way are of course, not protected against dust and damage.

FRAMING RUBBINGS
Small rubbings are framed just like pictures, either cut out and mounted on card or with card backings to hold them uncreased against the picture glass.

Big rubbings are difficult to frame because the weight of glass needs a fair-sized frame to support it, and wide frames just do not look well on rubbings. The best way round this is to panel the rubbing. Back it with $\frac{3}{8}$-inch chipboard, placing a sheet of white paper between chipboard and rubbing if it is on white paper. This is unnecessary if the rubbing is on coloured paper. Have a piece of glass cut exactly the same size as the chipboard. Get enough right-angled black plastic strip to frame the picture. Cut the strip to the right lengths, mitreing the corners. Bore small holes to take long blackheaded tacks or round-headed brass screws if you prefer them (screws make a stronger and safer job), in one side of each plastic strip. Lay the chipboard on the ground and put on it the plain white sheet, the rubbing and the glass in that order. Use Araldite, and plenty of it, to glue the plastic strip to the edges of the chipboard, all the way round. Then additionally tack or screw the strip into place as an added precaution. Screw two strong hanging plates to the chipboard, as the finished job will be very heavy. If it can be put up with the bottom edge supported in some way, all the better. The right-angled strip stuck and screwed to the chipboard is strong enough to take the weight of the glass, as no frame of comparable width would be.

MOUNTING RUBBINGS
Cut-out rubbings can be mounted on various materials, on to coloured card, direct on to walls or wooden panels, on hardboard panels covered with hessian, or on plywood panels. Plastic leather cloth mounted on hardboard or wood also makes a good backing for rubbings. All adhesives which soak into the paper of the rubbing stretch it and make it extremely

difficult to mount well. Small rubbings are not too difficult to cope_with, but it is necessary to lay both rubbing and mounting surface flat and use a roller to squeeze out air bubbles. The surplus adhesive will also squeeze out round the edges which can make quite a mess, so be careful. Aerosol spray adhesive which is an impact adhesive is by far the best I have come across both for mounting rubbings and for sticking material to boards and so on when making panels. The aerosol principle makes it very easy to use, as one can get the adhesive on to big surfaces far more quickly than with a brush or palette knife. The only difficult thing about impact adhesives is that both surfaces to be joined must have adhesive sprayed on to them, and must, after a few minutes, be brought together once and for all; there can be no stripping off again or sliding about of two parts to get things straight.

92 WALTER SEPTVANS, 1626
Ash-next-Sandwich, Kent
The light source was at one end of the brass. The foreshortening is due to the position of the camera, unavoidable without stepladders. (Wide angle 35mm lens used.)

It is essential to mark off final positions carefully before placing the rubbings on the mounts.

Foil rubbings can be mounted with the aerosol adhesive. Black grained plastic leather cloth makes an extremely effective backing for foil.

There are always problems about covering rubbings; non-reflective glass is very expensive but cannot be bettered. Perspex sheeting is also expensive, but has the advantage of being almost unbreakable, and capable of taking screws, so hanging and fixing plates can be used directly on the perspex without frames.

The enormous advantage of rubbings on cloth is that they can be attached directly to any surface or panel and need no cover to protect them. A gold rubbing on blue, for instance, tacked to a wood panelled wall with round-headed brass tacks, looks very fine. Or it can be held to the wall by flat strips of wood.

SCREEN PRINTING

If you have learned how to make screen prints, then you will have no difficulty preparing the screen and making prints using brass rubbings. If the techniques are unfamiliar to you, borrow the Batsford book by Anthony Kinsey, Introducing Screen Printing, from your local library. This will give you a lot of help, especially with the actual printing from the screen which cannot be gone into here. Permanent prints on cloth can be made from screens, but it seems rather pointless to do this for decorative purposes, rather than to use a rubbing itself. If you do wish to produce several copies of a rubbing for any reason, then this is one way to do it. Small rubbings can be reproduced on such things as scarves, skirts and tablecloths.

You will need a wooden frame with three layers of cotton organdie stretched tight without wrinkles and tacked to it. Make the screen about 2 inches bigger all round than the brass rubbing you wish to reproduce and then stick an edging of gum strip or PVC tape right round it to frame the printing area neatly. Dissolve photographic gelatine in hot water according to manufacturer's instructions and then paint it all over the organdie, using a soft new decorator's paint brush. Make sure that the surface is completely covered and has no air bubbles. Air bubbles show up later in the print. Allow the gelatine to dry hard, and in a darkened room coat the whole surface with potassium dichromate. As soon as it is dry, this chemical becomes light sensitive, so it must not be allowed to see the light. Store it in a dark cupboard overnight and by the next day it should be ready to use. Rub turpentine or thin lubricating oil all over the surface of the detail paper and the brass rubbing; this makes it less opaque so more light can get through to the screen for a clearer picture.

Then fix the rubbing to a sheet of clear glass slightly bigger than the wooden frame. Place the screen on a board which just fits inside the wooden frame, with the gelatined side up. Put the glass and the rubbing on top of that. Then, without moving the rubbing at all, expose the whole thing to a good light, either in a window or strong artificial light. About three to five minutes is enough and can be judged by the changing colour of the potassium dichromate where not covered by the rubbing. It goes from orange yellow to light brown. It takes a little experience to judge the exposure exactly.

Lift off the glass and the rubbing, and immediately wash off the screen with warm water. This removes the gelatine which was under the black parts of the rubbing. Put the screen aside to dry and then it is ready for use. Treat it gently and store it carefully.

PHOTOGRAPHING RUBBINGS

Photographs of brass rubbings, because they so drastically reduce their size, give them many uses. They make excellent Christmas and greetings cards and bookmarks. Framed sets of photographs are a good way to display rubbings. Photographs can be mounted on trays or small table tops under plate glass or to make decorative panels.

Perhaps the best use of photographs is to make compact records of your brass rubbings, or of the brasses themselves, and to record and enlarge detailed sections of brasses for study. Colour transparencies of brass rubbings can provide a way of looking at your work without having to unroll all the rubbings, and a far more convenient way of showing them to other people.

Rubbings are not all that easy to photograph successfully but, provided you have a fairly good camera and can do your own enlarging, you should be able to get quite good results. Because the production of very contrasty black and white prints is the object of the exercise, each print will need individual care, and there is not much future in taking photographs of rubbings and expecting a processing laboratory which is mass producing prints, to make very much of them. The shapes of the rubbings, usually long and narrow, mean that each negative will have to be masked differently for a start.

Rubbings are usually very big, and it is difficult, without a lot of studio lighting, to get even light over the whole surface indoors. So it is best to work out of doors on a bright day, but in hazy or indirect light, not in bright sunlight shining straight on to the rubbings. Because the slightest breeze will blow the rubbings about and cause ripples on the paper which will photograph as areas of light shadow, the rubbing must be firmly held down. A big picture window makes an excellent base, as the rubbings can be stuck firmly to it with small pieces of Sellotape X Failing this, you may have to get a large sheet of hardboard and paint it white and mount each rubbing on that to photograph it.

Flash can be used indoors, provided it is diffused across the rubbing and not used direct. A brolly flash set up on a tripod is excellent for this work. The inside of the open white umbrella reflects back the flash which points up into the middle of it, away from the subject, back over the subject as a diffused light. Calculate the aperture needed according to the instructions with your flash gun, measuring the distance from the light source to the subject from the centre point of the brolly. Set the flash up at an angle of at least 30 degrees and not more than 50 degrees from the rubbing. This ensures that the reflected light from the shiny black wax will not reach the camera, because it will largely bounce off at the same angle and miss the lens which should be set up exactly facing the centre of the rubbing. If the flash is set up right beside the camera, any reflection will come straight back into the lens.

Small rubbings and detail can be photographed with the normal lens, but a wide angle lens (35mm) is necessary to cope with big rubbings. The camera, either hand held or on a tripod must, as stated above, face the exact centre of the rubbing, or part of the rubbing to be photographed, if there is to be no distortion.

Use a fairly slow film, about 125 ASA which will give good contrast and fine grain. Take notes of the shutter speeds and apertures you use so that you find by experience which gives the best results. Print up the results to half plate size on white smooth glossy paper, using Bromide hard (grade 3 or even 4). Use contrast developer. This should produce black and white pictures with no half tones which is what you need. Of course, for special jobs you may prefer semi matt or matt paper to give a less obviously photographic result, but some contrast will be lost.

Colour photographing of rubbings is far best done out of doors, following the exposures recommended by the makers of the film for the weather conditions, or using an exposure meter to get really good results. Point the meter at the dark parts of the picture, as the white paper will give too high a reading, and you may underexpose.

Photographs of black and white rubbings reproduce them exactly as they are – negative images. To get film which can be printed up to produce positive pictures in which the brass is white and the engraved lines and background black, the original film is printed again on film, not on paper, processed and then used for printing on paper in the usual way. Photographers with a good dark room who do their own developing will not find this too difficult. However, there is another way for those who only do their own enlarging. Photograph the rubbings on colour reversal film thus getting transparencies of a black and white subject. Use these transparencies in your enlarger just like ordinary negatives, and you will get excellent positive black and white prints of your rubbings. Because the black is so dense on the colour transparency it will print up vivid white without any veiling. Facial characteristics appear much more lifelike on a positive print. The rather prissy, mealymouthed faces of many of the women, few of whom look beautiful or even happy are all too clearly revealed. Perhaps this can be blamed on the engraver and not on the subject.

93 CHRISTINA PHELYP, 1470
Herne, Kent
Uneven result from flash held at one side of subject. Foreshortening is caused by camera position at one end of the brass. (Wide angle lens 35mm used.)

PHOTOGRAPHING BRASSES

Many of the problems are the same as those encountered when photographing rubbings, but are made more difficult by the fixed position and poor lighting of the subjects. To take a photograph of a big brass set in the floor of a church, without distortion, it is necessary to get square above it, and this is usually impossible without scaffolding or hanging oneself from the ceiling. Small brasses and murals are not so difficult as one can stand on a chair or steps to one side of the brass and hold the camera out over it *(fig. 92)*.

It is almost essential to use a wide angle lens, except for the smallest brasses. 35mm will cover a wide area without distortion. Whether standing above the brass or at one end of it one can get the whole brass in picture *(fig. 93)*.

Using electronic flash at a 60th second the aperture will probably be f8 or f11, according to the power of the flash and the distance of the subject from the light source, and this aperture will give a reasonable depth of field inside which the brass will be in focus. Using a bigger aperture the whole length of the brass could not be in focus. Working from directly above this problem is not so great.

If the flash gun is attached to the camera

94a and b THOMAS BOYS, 1562
Upper Deal, Kent

A fine mural brass in its original casement. On thin English brass, it has worn well because of its position. The face is a sensitive portrait, but what a pity a screw has been driven through his forehead. Thomas Boys was for two years Mayor of Calais, was captain of Deal Castle, and was with Henry VIII at Boulogne. These two photographs show clearly how differing angles affect the result. Both were taken from the same distance at the same aperture, one frontally to catch all the reflection, the other from one side.

the result will be good, but one end of the brass will be better lit than the other if you are standing at one end *(fig. 92)*. The result may be better if you get an assistant to hold the flash gun halfway along the length of the brass, or if you set up the flash using a brolly diffuser to spread the light evenly over the subject. It is extremely hard to give any rules of thumb, and experimentation will provide you with differing results from which you can decide what type of picture you like best.

It is possible working close to the subject with the flash gun on the camera to get results like *figs 94a and 94b* where the light has come straight back to show the metal up as very bright and the engraving as dark lines *(fig. 70)*. If the brass has been polished, extremely bright reflections may come back into the camera. If the lighting is too even the photographs will be dull. Brasses are a little dull to the eye, and some highlights and reflection can give, photographically, a far better impression of a metallic surface than does too flat a picture.

COLOUR PHOTOGRAPHY OF BRASSES

There will rarely be enough light in a church for good colour photography at a shutter speed at which the camera can be hand held. It will have to be set up on a tripod and an exposure meter used to get the right time exposure. Some experience is needed before you get good results.

Keep careful records of all exposures, apertures, position of flash, and distance from subject and so on, so that good results can be repeated. Be prepared to expose a lot of film, both black and white and colour. You may find in the long run that the photographing of brasses is just as interesting and engrossing (and far more difficult) than rubbing brasses. As will be seen from *fig. 16* photography brings up a lot of detail in indents – enough for a lifetime's study – but that is another subject.

COUNTY LISTS

The lists beginning overleaf note only about a quarter of the brasses which exist, as exhaustive lists would take up the whole book. It is intended to help the beginner to find some good brasses to rub. The serious rubber should get either the Victoria and Albert Museum catalogue, or the Le Strange book, detailed in the Bibliography. These are purely and simply lists. Although there are a few omissions in the V. & A. book, it is so good, easy to use, and so well illustrated that I find it indispensible. It is also cheap!

The lists here have been simplified to save space and for easy reference. Each entry gives the type of brass and its date. As you become conversant with brasses you will find that this is all the basic information you need to give you a rough idea, before visiting the church, of what you may find.

M   Military
W   Women, either wives or ladies by themselves
C   Civilian man, be he merchant, lawyer, or esquire
E   Ecclesiastic, either male or female, or religious subject such as cross, or saint
Ch Child
G   Gruesome – shrouds, skeletons etc.
I   Inscriptions and shields of arms
P   After the date, indicates that the brass is a palimpsest

COUNTY LISTS

BEDFORDSHIRE

Ampthill C,W,1450. W,1485. C,W,1506. M,1532. Aspley Guise E,1410. M,1501. Bedford, St. Paul M,W,1573. Bromham M,2W,1435,P. Caddington C,W,1505. C,2W,1518. Cardington M,2W,1540. M,W,1638. Clifton M,W,1528. Cople C,W,1410. M,1415. M,W,1435,1507,1556. C,W,1544,1563. Dunstable C,W,1516. 2C,W,1640. Eaton Bray W,1558. Elstow W,1427. E,1520. Eyeworth C,W,1624. Holwell E,1515. Luton, St. Mary C,1415. W,1490. M,2W,1513. E,1510. W,1515. Marston Mortaine E,1420. M,W,1451. I,1506. Shillington E,1400,1485. Turvey C,1480. E,1500. W,1606. Wymington C,W,1391. W,1407. M,1430. E,1510. Yelden E,1433. C,1628.

BERKSHIRE

Appleton G,1518. Ashbury C,1360. E,1409,1448. Binfield E,1361,I,1558,P. Blewbury E,1496. M,2W,1515. M,W,1523,1548,P. Bray M,2W,1378. C,1475. C,2W,1490. C,W,1610,1620. Childrey M,W,1444. E,1480. C,W,1480. E,1490. G,1507. M,W,1514. C,G,1516. C,W,1520. E,1529. Cookham C,W,1458,1503,1577,P. M,W,1510,1527. Coxwell, Great C,1509. W,1510. Denchworth M,W,1516,1562,P. 1567. Hanney, West E,1370. M,1557,1599. C,2W,1592. M,2W,1602. C,W,1611. Lambourn C,W,1406. 2C,1410. M,1485. C,W,1619. Marcham M,W,1540. Reading, St. Lawrence C,W,1415,1584. C,1538,P. Shottesbrooke E,C,1370. W,1401. M,1511. C,3W,1567. Sonning M,1434. C,W,1549. W,1575,1589. Ch 1627. Sparsholt E,1353. C,1495,1602. W,1510. Swallowfield W,1466. M,W,1554. Wantage E,1370. M,1414. E,1512. C,2W,1522. W,1619. Windsor, St. George's Chapel, many fine brasses, but no rubbing. Wittenham, Little E,1433. C,1454. W,1472. C,1483. C,W,1585. M,1588. Ch,1683.

BUCKINGHAMSHIRE

Amersham C,W,1430,1439,1521. C,1450. Ch,1623. Burnham C,W,1500,1563,P. C,3W,1581,P. Chalfont St. Giles E,1470. W,1510. C,2W,1560,P. M,W,1558. M,2W,1570. Chalfont St. Peter M,W,1446,1446. E,1545,P. Chenies C,2W,1469. M,W,1484. E,1494. W,1510,1511,1524. Chicheley M,W,1558,P. G,1560. Denham M,2W,1494. E,1540. W,1545,P reverse E. E,1560. Dinton M,W,1424,1539,1628. C,W,1486,1558,P. M,1551,P. Drayton Beauchamp M,1368,1375. E,1531. Edlesborough E,1395. M,3W,1540,P. C,W,1592. Ellesborough M,W,1544,P. Eton College Chapel, many Civilians and Inscriptions. Halton C,W,1553,P. Hambledon C,1457. C,W,1497, 1600. W,1500. C,2W,1634. Hampden, Great M,W,1525. M,2W,1553,P. Hedgerley C,W,1498. W,1540,P. Penn G,1540. M,W,1597,P. 1638,1641. W,1640. Pitstone W,1320. Quainton W,1360. E,1422,1485. W,1509,1593. C,1510. Shalston W,1540. Slapton E,1462. C,2W,1519. Soulbury C,W,1502. C,1516. Stokenchurch M,1410,1415. Stoke Poges M,W,1425. C,W,1577. Swanbourn C,W,1626. Taplow E,C,1350. C,W,G,1455. M,2W,1540,P. Thornborough C,W,1420. Thornton M,3W,1472. W,1557. Tyringham M,1484. W,1508. Twyford E,1413. M,1550,P. Waddesdon M,1490. E,1543. G,1548. M,W,1561,P. Winchendon, Over E,1502. I,1558. Wooburn C,1488. C,W,1500. E,1519. G,1520. Ch,1642. Wootton Underwood C,W,1587. Wraysbury M,1488. C,1512.

CAMBRIDGESHIRE

Balsham E,1401,1462. M,1480. Burwell E,1542,P. Cambridge: St. Benet E,1442. St. Mary the Less E,1436,1500. St. John's Coll. E,1414,1430. King's Coll. E,1496,1507,1528, 1558.I,1559. Trinity Hall E,1517. E,1530. C,1598. I,1611,1645,1659. Croxton C,1589. Ely Cathedral E,1554,1614. I,1621. Fulbourn E,1390,1391,1477. W,1470. Hildersham E,C,W,1408. M,1427. M,1466. G,1530. Horseheath M,1365. C,1552. Impington M,W,1505. Isleham M,W,1451. M,2W,1484. C,W,1574, P. Milton C,W,1553,P. 1660. Shelford, Little M.W,1405. E,1480. Swaffham Prior M,W,1462. C,W,1515,1521,1530. C.1638. Trumpington Sir Roger de Trumpington 1289. Westley Waterless M,W,1325.

88

CHESHIRE
Chester, Holy Trinity I,1545,P. Macclesfield C,1506. Over M,1510. Wilmslow M,W,1460.
CORNWALL
Blisland E,1410. St. Budock C,W,1567. Callington C,W,1465. Colan C,W,1572,1575. St. Columb
Major M,2W,1545. M,W,1633. Constantine C,W,1574,P. 1616. Crowan E,1420. C,W,1490,1550,
P. St. Erme C,W,1596. Illogan M,W,1603. St. Just E,1520. Lanteglos-by-Fowey M,W,1440,1525.
Launceston W,1620. Mawgan-in-Pyder E,1420. W,1578,1580,P. C,1580. St. Mellion M,W,1551,P.
St. Michael Penkevil M,1497. E,1515. C,1619. M,1640. W,1622. Quethiock C,W,1471,1631.
Stratton M,2W,1561. Tintagel W,1430.
CUMBERLAND
Carlisle Cathedral E,1496,1616. Edenhall M,W,1458.
DERBYSHIRE
Ashbourne I,1241. C,1538. Dronfield 2E,1399. C,W,1578. Edensor M,1570. Etwall W,1512.
M,2W,1557. Hathersage M,W,1463,1500,1560. Morley M,W,1453. M,2W,1470. M,3W,1481.
M,W,1525,1558. Mugginton M,W,1475. Norbury C,W,1538,P. Sawley M,W,1467,1478.
C,W,1510. Tideswell E,1462. C,W,1500. E,1579. Walton-on-Trent E,1492.
DEVONSHIRE
Bigbury W,1440,1460. Dartmouth, St. Savior M,2W,1408. W,1470. C,1637. Exeter Cathedral
M,1409. E,1413. St. Giles-in-the-Wood W,1430,1592,1610. Harford M,1566. C,W,1639. Petrock-
stow M,W,1591. Shillingford M,W,1499. Stoke Fleming C,W,1391. Stoke-in-Teignhead E,1370.
I,1641. Yealmpton M,1508. I,1580,P.
DORSETSHIRE
Bere Regis C,W,1596. Evershot E,1524. Fleet M,W,1603,1612. Knowle, Church M,2W,1572.
Milton Abbey M,1565. Piddlehinton I,1562,P. E,1617. Pimperne W,1694. Purse Caundle M,1500.
W,1527. E,1536. Shapwick W,1440. E,1520. Thorncombe C,W,1437. Wimborne Minster. St.
Ethelred 1440. Yetminster M,W,1531.
DURHAM
Auckland, St. Andrew E,1380,1581. Houghton-le-Skerne W,1592. Houghton-le-Spring W,1587.
Sedgefield 2G,1500.
ESSEX
Arkesden M,1439. Aveley M,1370. Ch,1583,1520. I,1584. 2Ch,1588. Bardfield, Great W,1584.
Barking E,1480,1485. C,W,1493,P. 1596. Ch,1530. Bowers, Gifford M,1348. Braxted, Little
M,2W,1508. Brightlingsea C,W,1496. W,1505,1514. C,2W,1521,P. C,W,1525. 2W,1536.
C,1578. Bromley E,1432. Chigwell E,1631. Crishall M,W,1380. W,1450. C,W,1480. Clavering
C,W,1480,1591,1593. Colchester, St. Peter C,W,1530,1572. 2C,W,1553. C,1563. C,2W,1610.
Corringham E,1340. C,1460. Cressing W,1610. Dagenham 2C,W,1479. Easton, Little E,1420.
M,W,1483. Faulkbourn M,1576. W,1598. Finchingfield M,W,1523. Gosfield C,1440. Halstead
M,2W,1420. W,1604. Harlow M,W,1430. C,1559,1602,1615. C,W,1490,1518. Hatfield Peverel
C,W,1572. Hempstead C,1475,1480. C,W,1475,1498,1518,1530. Horkesley, Little 2M,1412.
G,1502. 2M,W,1549,P. Hornchurch C,W,1591,1604. 2W,1602. Ilford, Little Schoolboy,1517.
W,1630. Ingrave W,1466. M,4W,1528. Lambourne C,W,1546,P. Latton M,W,1467,1490.
W,1604. C,W,1600. Leigh 2C,Ws,1453. C,W,1632,1640. Littlebury C,1480,1520. E,1510. C,W,
1510. W,1578,1624. Nettleswell C,W,1522,1607. Okendon M,W,1502. C,1532. Okendon South
M,1400. W,1602. Pebmarsh M,1323. Roydon M,W,1471. M,2W,1521. C,1570. M,1589. Runwell
M,W,1587. Saffron Walden E,1430,1480. 2W,1480. W,1500,1530. C,W,1510,1530. C,1530.
Stanford Rivers Chrysom 1492. M,W,1503,1540. Stifford E,1378. G,1480. C,W,1504,1622.
W,1627,1630. Stock M,1574. Stondon Massey C,W,1570,1573,P. Terling C,W. C,2W,1584,P.
Tilty M,W,1520,1562. W,1590. Tolleshunt Darcy M,W,1420. W,1535,P. M,1540,P. Upminster
W,1455. C,1530,1545,P. W,1555,1636. M,1591. Waltham Abbey C,W,1565,1576. Wimbish
M,W,1347. Writtle M,W,1500,1513. C,4W,1510. W,1524,1592. C,W,1576,1606,1609. Wyvenhoe
M,1507. E,1535. W,1537,P.
GLOUCESTERSHIRE
Bisley W,1515. Bristol: St. John C,W,1478. St. Mary Redcliff C,1439. E,1460,P. M,2W,1475.
C,W,1480. C,W,1522. Chipping Campden C,W,1401,1450,1467. C,3W,1484. Cirencester
M,1438. E,1478,1480. 12 brasses to wool-merchants, from 1400 to 1626. Deerhurst C,W,1400.
W,1520,1525. Dyrham M,W,1401. Fairford M.W,1500. M,2W,1534. Gloucester St. Mary de
Crypt 2W,1519. C,W,1544. Leckampton C,W,1598. Minchinhampton C,W,1500,1519. G,1510.
Newland M,W,1443. Northleach 7 brasses of wool-merchants and wives, 1400,1447,1458, 1485,

1490,1501, 1526. E,1530. Rodmarton C,1461. Wormington W,1605. Wootton-under-Edge M,W,1392.

HAMPSHIRE
Candover, Brown C,W,1490. Crondall E,1381. M,1563. G,1641. Eversley E,1502. Havant E,1413. Headbourne Worthy C,1434. Kimpton M,2W,1522. Odiham C,W,1480. E,1498. W,1504,1522. C,1535. M,1540,P. Ch,1636. Ringwood E,1416. Sherborne St. John C,W,1360. M,1488,1492. M,2W,1492. M,1540. Sombourne, King's 2C,1380. Southwick M,W,1548,P. Stoke Charity M,1482. M,W,1483. Thruxton M,1425. Warnborough M,1512. Whitchurch C,W,1603. Winchester, St. Cross E,1382,1493,1518.

HEREFORDSHIRE
Clehonger M,W,1470. Hereford Cathedral E,1360,1386,1428,1434,1476,1529. M,W,1435. M,2W, 1514. Ledbury E,1410. M,1490,1614. Ludford M,W,1554,P. Marden W,1614.

HERTFORDSHIRE
Aldbury C,1478. M,W,1547. Aldenham 5C brasses 3W,1520–1535. G,1547. Aspenden C,W,1500. M,W,1508. Baldock W,1410. C,W,1420,1480. G.1480. Berkhampstead, Great C,W,1356. M,1365. W,1370, E,1400. C,1485. G,1520. Broxbourne E,1470,1510. M,W,1473. C,1531. Buckland W,1451. E,1478. C,1499. Cheshunt E,1448. C,W,1449. W,1453,1502,1609. Clothall E,1404,1519, 1541,1602. W,1578,P. Digswell M,W,1415. M,1442. G,1484. C,W,1495,1530,P. Essendon C,W,1588. Hadham Great E,1420. C,W,1582. C,2W,1610. Hadham, Little E,1470. M,W,1485. Hemel Hempstead M,W,1390. Hinxworth C,W,1450,1487. Hitchin 6C with W,1421–1550. 4G,1480–1490. E,1498. Hunsdon G,1495. C,1591. Kimpton W,1450. Knebworth E,1414. M,2W, 1582. Mymms, North E,1361. W,1458. M,1488. C,W,1490. M,W,1560. Pelham, Furneux C,W, 1420. M,W,1518. Radwell C,W,1487. C,2W,1516. W,1602. St. Alban's Abbey E,1360,1400,P. 4E,1450,1470,1470,1521. M,W,1468,1519. M,1480. C,W,1411. C,1465,1470. St. Alban's, St. Michael C,W,1380. M,1380. E,1400. Sawbridgeworth M,W,1437,1600. M,1480. C,2W,1470. G,1484. W,1527,1600. Standon C,1460. C,M,1477. M,1557,P. Walkerne C,W,1480,1583,P. 1636. Ware W,1400,1454. C,2W,1470. Watford C,1415. W,1416. 3C,1613. Watton M,1361. E,1370. C,1450,1470. W,1455,1545. M,1514. Wormley C,W,1479,1490,1598. Wyddiall C,W,1546,P. W,1575.

HUNTINGDONSHIRE
Diddington M,W,1505. W,1513. Offard Darcy M,2W,1440,P. E,1530. Sawtry All Saints M,W, 1404. Stilton C,W,1606. 2C,1618.

ISLE OF WIGHT
Calbourne M,1380. E,1652. Freshwater M,1367. Kingston C,1535. Shorwell E,1518. 2W,1619.

KENT
Addington M,1378. M,W,1409,1470. M,1415,1445. E,1446. Ash next Sandwich W,1455,1455. C,W,1525. M,W,1602. C,W,1642. Aylesford M,W,1426. Beckenham M,2W,1552. W,1563. Bexley Hunting-horn etc, 1410. C,1513. Biddenden 2C,W,1520. M,W,1566. C,1572,1593. C,W,1628,1641. C,2W,1584,1598,1609. Birchington C,1449,1454. W,1518,1528,1533. E,1523. Bobbing M,W,1420. M,1420. W,1496. Boughton-under-Blean C,W,1508,1591. M,1587. Brabourn M,1433,1524. W,1450,1528. Canterbury St. Martin C,W,1587. M,1591. Chart, Great C,1470,1680. C,W,1485,1500,1565,P. C,5W,1499. M,2W,1513. Chartham Sir Robert de Septvans, 1306. E,1416,1454,1508. W,1530. Cobham W,1315,1375,1380,1395,1433,1506. M,1354,1365, 1405,1407,1402. M,W,1529. E,1418,1402,1450,1498,1420,1447. M,1402. Dartford C,W,1402, 1496. C,2W,1590. C,1508. W,1454,1464,1590,1612. Deal, Upper C,W,1508. M,1562. Chrysom, 1606. Eastry M,W,1590. Edenbridge C,1558. Erith C,1425. C,W,1435,1511. W,1471. M,W,1537. Faversham M,1414,1500,1580,1610. E,1480,1531. C,W,1533. C,2W,1533. Goodnestone C,W, 1507,1558,1568. Goudhurst M,1424,1520. M,W,1481. Graveney W, son,1360. M,1381, C,W,1436. Halling, Lower W,in bed,1587. Hardres, Upper E,1405. Headcorn Child 1636. Herne M,W,1430. E,1450. W,1470,1539. C,2W,1604. Hever W,1419. M,1538. C,1584. Hoo, St. Werburgh E,1406, 1412. C,1430,1446. M,W,1465. W,1615. C,W,1640. Horsmonden E,1340. W,1604. Horton Kirby W,1460. C,W,1595. Lullingstone M,1487. W,1533,1544. Lydd E,1420. C,W,1430,1557,1566. C,1508,1520,1587,1590. W,1590. Maidstone All Saints C,W,1593,1640. Malling C,W,1479. E,1522. Margate St. John C,1431,1442. Heart & Scrolls,1433. C,W,1441. M,1445. G,1446. E,1515. M,1590. I,Ship,1615. Mereworth M,1366. C,W,1479. C,1542. Milton-next-Sittingbourne M,1470. M,W,1496. W,1529. Minster-in-Sheppy M,1330,P. W,1335. Newington-next-Hythe W,1480. G,W,1501. E,1501. C,3W,1522. C,1600. M,W,1630. Northfleet E,1375,1391. M,W,1433. Otterden M,1408,1502,1508. W,1488,1606. Pluckley M,1440. W,1526. M,W,1610. Preston near Faversham

M,W,1442. M,1459. W,1612. Rochester, St. Margaret E, 1465,P. Saltwood E,1370. M,W,1437. E,Heart,1496. Seal M,1395. C,1577,P. Sheldwich M,W,1437.1426. G,1431. Southfleet W,1414. C,W,1420. E,1456. G,1520. C,W,1520. Stone E,1408. Sutton M,W,1629. Ulcombe M,1419,1442. M,W,1470. Upchurch C,W,1350. Westerham C,W,1529,P. C,1531. C,2W,1533,1557,P. 2C,1545. E,1567. Wickham, East C,W,1325. M,3W,1568. Wickham, West E,1407,1515. Woodchurch E,1330. M,1558. Wrotham C,W,1498. C,1500. M,W,1512,1525,1611. W,1615.

LANCASHIRE
Childwall M,W,1524. Eccleston E,1510. Manchester Cathedral E,1458,1515. M,W,1460. M,1540,P. C,W,1607,1629. Middleton E,1522. M,W,1510,1650. C,W,1618. 2M,W,1531. Ormskirk M,1500. Preston C,1623. Sefton W,1528. M,2W,1568,1570. Whalley Abbey M,W,1515. Winwick M,1492, 1527.

LEICESTERSHIRE
Bottesford E,1404,1440. Donington Castle M,W,1458. Sheepshed M,W,1592. Sibson E,1532. Stapleford M,W,1492. Stokerston M,W,1467,1493. Wanlip M,W,1393.

LINCOLNSHIRE
Althorpe E,1360. Barton-on-Humber W,1380. C,1433. Bigby W,1520. E,W,1632. Boston C,1398, 1659. E,1400. C,2W,1400. C,W,1470. Broughton M,W,1390. Buslingthorpe M,1310. Croft M,1310. Edenham E,1500. Evedon C,W,1630. Grainthorpe E,1380. Gunby, St. Peter M,W,1552,P. C,1419. Hainton C,W,1435. M,W,1553. Harrington W,1480. M,W,1585. Horncastle M,G,1519,P. Ingoldmells C,1520. Irnham M,1390,1440. Kelsey, South M,W,1410. Laughton M,1549,P. Linwood C,W,1419. C,1421. Norton Disney M,W,1578. M,2W,1578. Ormsby, South W,1410. M,W,1482. Scrivelsby M,1545. Spilsby W,1391. M,W,1400. Stamford, All Saints C,W,1460,1460, 1475,1500. W,1471. E,1508. Tattershall C,1411. M,1455. W,1479,1497. E,1456,1510,1519. Theddlethorpe, All Saints M,1424. Wrangle C,W,1503.

MIDDLESEX
London (anticlockwise starting in the east, north of the Thames. E.8. Hackney, St. John Bapt. E,1521. M,4W,1562. N.9 Edmonton, All Saints 2C,W,1500. C,W,1523,1616. N.1. Islington, St. Mary M,W,1540,P,1546,P. N.3. Finchley, St. Mary C,W,1609. C,3W,1610. W,1609,1487. E.C.2. Bishopsgate, Great St. Helen C,W,1465,1495. E,1482,1500. M,1510,1514. W,1535. E.C.3. All Hallows, Tower Hill W,C,1437,1477,1533. E,1500. C,1498,1591. C,2W,1518. M,W,1546,P,1560. M,1552,P,1556,P. E.C.4. St. Dunstan-in-the-West, Fleet C,W,1530. S.W.1. Westminster Abbey E,1395,1397,1498,1561. W,1399. M,1438,1483,1505. S.W.3. Chelsea Old Church W,1555. M,W, 1625. S.W.6. Fulham All Saints W,1555. W.5. Ealing, St. Mary C,W,1490. S.W.15. Wandsworth All Saints C,1420. Drayton, West C,1520. W,1529. C,W,1581,P. Greenford, Great E,1450,1521. W,1480,1544. Hadley 2W,1442. C,W,1500,1518,1614. W,1504. Harefield W,1444. C,1528. M,W, 1537,P,1537. C,W,1545. Harlington E,1419. M,W,1545,P. Harrow M,1370,1390. E,1442,1460, 1468. C,3W,1488. M,W,1479,P,1592. C,1603. Hayes E,1370. M,1456. M,W,1576. Hillingdon M,W,1509. M,1528. C,W,1579. C,1599. Ickenham C,1580,1582. M,W,1584. Isleworth M,1450. E,1561. C,1590. Northolt M,1452. M,W,1560. E,1610. Ruislip C,W,1593,1574. C,1600. Willesden C,W,1492. W,1505,1550,1609. E,1517. M,2W,1585.

MONMOUTHSHIRE
Matherne C,W,1590. Usk I,1421.

NORFOLK
Aldborough M,1481. W,1485. C,1490. Aylsham E,1490. C,W,1490,1500. G,1499,1507. Bawburgh C,W,1500. E,1505,1531. G,1660. Beechamwell E,1385,1430. Blickling C,1360. M,1401. C,W,1454. W,1458,1485,1512. Child,1479. Buckenham, Old Crane with scroll,1500. E,1520. Burnham Thorpe M,1420. Bylaugh M,W,1471. Cley C,1450,1500. C,G,1512. E,1520. I,1578,P. Creake, North C,1500. Ditchingham C,W,1490. C,son,1505. Elsing M,1347. Erpingham, 1415. Felbrigg C,W, and M,W,1380. M,1416,1608. W,1480,1606. Fransham M,1414. G,1500. Frenze M,1475,P, 1510. W,1519,1521,1551. G,1520. Halvergate W,1540,P. Hellesdon C,W,1370. E,1389. Holme-next-the-Sea C,W,1405. Hunstanton C,W,1480. M,1506. Ketteringham W,1470. M,W,1499. G,1530. Loddon E,1462. 2G,1546. M,1561. C,W,1609. Lynn, St. Margt. M,W,1349. M,2W,1364. Merton M,2W,1520. M,1562. Methwold M,1367. Narburgh C,W,1496,1545. M,1545,1581. M,W,1561. Necton W,1372,1596. E,1583. C,1528. C,W,1532. Newton Flotman 3M,1571. Norwich: St. George Colegate C,W,1472. St. Giles C,W,1432,1436. E,1499. St. John Maddermarket C,W,1412,1472,1476,1525,1524,1558,P. W,1506. St. Laurence C,1436. E,1437,1483. G,1452. St. Stephen E,1546,P,1545. C,1460. 2C,1513. C,W,1513. Ormesby, Great W,1538,P. M,1529. Paston C,W,1582,P. Reedham W,1474. I,1502,P. C,1536. Rougham C,W,1472. M,W,

1510. 2 Chrysoms,1510. C,2W,1586. Salle C,1420. C,W,1440,1441. 2W,1453. G,1454. Shern-
bourne M,W,1458. Southacre M,W,1384. E,1584. Upwell E,1430,1435. C,1621. Wiveton E,1512.
G,1540. C,W,1597. Worstead E,1404. C,1500,1520.

NORTHAMPTONSHIRE
Ashby Castle E,1401. Ashby St. Ledger C,W,1416. M,W,1494,1500,1553. E,1510. Ashton C,W,
1584. Blakesly M,1416. Blisworth M,W,1503. Brampton-by-Dingley M,W,1420. M,1476.
Charwelton C,W,1490,1490. M,W,1541,P. Cotterstock E,1420. Deene M,2W,1584. C,W,1586.
M,W,1606. Dodford M,W,1414,1422. W,1637. Easton Neston M,W,1552,P. Fawsley M,1516.
M,W,1557. Greens Norton M,W,1462. W,1490. Heyford, Lower M,W,1487. Higham Ferrers
E,1337,1400,1498. E,1523. C,W,1425,1504. C,1518,1540,1540. Heart,1500. Lowick M,W,1467.
Marholm M,W,1534. Newton-by-Geddington C,W,1400. W,1604. Rothwell E,1361. C,W,1514.
Sudborough C,W,1415. Wappenham M,1460. C,W,1479. M,W,1500,1500. Warkworth M,1412,
1420,1454. W,1420,1430. Welford M,3W,1585.

NORTHUMBERLAND
Newcastle-upon-Tyne, All Saints C,W,1411.

NOTTINGHAMSHIRE
Clifton M,1478,1491. M,W,1587. Hickling E,1521. Holme Pierrepont W,1390. Markham W,1419.
Newark C,1361,1540. C,1557. Strelley M,W,1487. Wollaton M,W,1471.

OXFORDSHIRE
Adderbury M,W,1460. W,1508. Bampton E,1420,1500. C,1633. Brightwell Baldwin C,W,1439.
Brightwell Salome E,1492. C,1549. Broughton C,1414. Burford C,W,1437,1614. Cassington
E,1414. G,1590. Charlton-on-Otmoor E,1476,P. Checkendon C,1404,P. E,1430. Chinnor E,1320,
1361,1388 and 6 others mutilated 1390–1514. M,2W,1385. M,W,1386. Chipping Norton C,W,
1450,1451,1484,1467. W,1503,1507,1530. Dorchester M,1417. E,1510. W,1490. C,W,1513.
M,W,1436. P,1518. E,1458,1467,1470,1517. Harpsden M,1460,1620. M,W,1480. E,1511.
Haseley, Gt. E,1494. G,1497. W,1581. Mapledurham M,1395. Newnham Murren E,1593. Noke
C,W,1598. Nuffield C,1360. Oxford: St. Aldate 2C,1607. C,1612,1637. St. Cross, Holywell
W,1622,1625. Christ Church Cath. C,1450,1452. E,1557. Students 1578,P,1584,1587,1588,1602,
1613. Magdalen Coll. 10C,1478–1523. E,1480,1480,1515,1558,P. Merton Coll. E,1322,1351,1471,
1519. C,1400,1445. New Coll. E,1417,1526,1507 and 12 E,1403–1521. C,1510,1592,1619,1601.
Queen's Coll. C,1477. E,1518,1616,1616. St. John's Coll. C,1571,1578,1573,1577. Rotherfield
Greys M,1387. Shipton-under-Wychwood G,1548,P. Somerton M,W,1552,P. Stanton Harcourt
2C,1460. W,1516. E,1519. Stoke Lyne C,W,1535,1582. Tew, Great M,W,1410. C,W,1513.
Thame 2M,2W,1420. M,1460,1539. C,W,1500,1502,1503,1508. C,1543,P,1597. Waterperry
W,1370. M,W,1540,P. Whitchurch M,W,1420. E,1455,1610. Witney C,2W,1500. C,1606.

RUTLAND
Casterton, Little M,W,1410.

SHROPSHIRE
Acton Burnell M,1382. Adderley E,1390. M,W,1560,P. Edgmond C,W,1533. Harley M,W,1475.
Ightfield W,1495. C,1497. Tong M,W,1467. E,1510,1517.

SOMERSETSHIRE
Banwell C,W,1480,1554. E,1503. Beckington M,W,1485. C,W,1505. Burnett C,W,1575. Hutton
M,W,1496,1528. Ilminster M,W,1440,1618. Luccombe C,1615. Petherton, South M,W,1430.
W,1442. St. Decumans M,W,1571,1596. M,1676. Shepton Mallet M,W,1649. Swainswick C,1439.
Wedmore M,1630. Wells Cathedral E,1460,1626. C,1618. Yeovil E,1460. C,W,1519.

STAFFORDSHIRE
Audley M,1385. C,1628. Clifton Campville W,1360,P. Horton C,W,1589. Kinver M,2W,1528.
Norbury C,1360. Okeover M,W,1538,P. Standon E,1420. Trentham M,W,1591.

SUFFOLK
Acton Sir Robt de Bures,1315. W,1435. M,1528. C,W,1589. C,1598. Aldeburgh C,1519. W,1520,
1570. C,W,1601,1606,1612,1635. Barrow M,2W,1570. Barsham M,1415. Bradley, Little C,W,
1510,1584,1605. M,1530. M,W,1612. Brundish E,1360. M,1599. M,W,1560. W,1570. Youth,1570.
Burgate, M,1409. Bury St. Edmunds, St. Mary C,W,1480. E,1514. Depden 2M,2W,1572.
Easton M,1425,1584. W,1601. Euston C,W,1480,1520. W,1520. M,W,1530. Gorleston M,1320.
Hawstead Boy, 1500. Girl, 1530. W,1530. M,2W,1557. Ipswich, St. Mary Tower C,1475. C,2W,
1500. 2C,W,1506. C,2W,1525. Ixworth C,W,1567. Lavenham C,W,G,1486. C,W,1560. Chry-
som,1631. Letheringham M,1389. Long Melford W,1420. C,1420. 2W,1480. M,1577. C,2W,1615.
C,3W,1624. Mendham W,1615. C,1616,1634. Mendlesham M,1417. Orford 12C with W 1480–

1640. C,1580,P. Playford M,1400. Ringsfield M,W,1595. Rougham M,W,1405. Sotterley M,1480, 1572,1630. M,W,1479. W,1578. Stoke by Nayland W,1400,1535. M,1408. Waldingfield, Little C,W,1506. M,W,1526. W,1530. C,1544. Wenham, Little M,W,1514. Wrentham C,1400. M,1593. Yoxford M,W,1428. G,1485. C,1613. W,1618.

SURREY
Addington M,1540. C,W,1544. Beddington W,1414,1507. C,W,1430,1432. M,1437. Betchworth E,1533. Bletchingley W,1470. E,1510. C,W,1541. Bookham, Great W,1433,1597. C,W,1598. C,1668. Byfleet E,1480. Carshalton M,W,1490. E,1493. M,1497. W,1524. Cheam C,1390,1390, 1459. C,W,1458,1452. M,1480,P. Cobham E,1500. M,1560,P. Cranleigh E,1503,1507. Crowhurst M,1450,1460. Ditton, Thames M,W,1599. 2C,W,1580,P. C,W,1582,1587,1587,1590. Ewell W,1519,1521. 2W,C,1577. Horley W,1516,P. C,1510. Horsell C,1603,1603. C,W,1519. Horsley, East C,1390. E,1478. C,W,1498. Lingfield W,1375,1420,1420,1450. M,1403,1417. E,1445,1458, 1469,1503. Merstham C,W,1463. 2W,1473. M,1498. M,W,1507. Ch,1587. Mickleham C,W,1513. Oakwood M,1431. Ockham E,1376. M,W,1483. Peper-Harrow W,1487,1621. E,1487. Richmond C,W,1591. Shere E,1412. C,1512. C,W,1516. W,1520. M,1525. Stoke d'Abernon Sir John d'Aubernon,1277,1327. W,1464. Chrysom,1516. C,W,1592. Thorpe C,W,1578,P,1583,P. Walton-on-Thames C,W,1587,P.

SUSSEX
Amberley M,1424. Ardingly C,W,1500. M,W,1504,1510. W,1633. Ch,1634. Arundel E,1382,1419, 1450,1474,1455. M,W,1430. M,1465. Battle M,1426,1435. E,1430. W,1590. C,1615. Broadwater E,1432,1445. Burton M,1520. W,1558. Buxted E,1408. Chichester Cathedral E,1500. C,W,1592. Clapham M,W,1526,1550,1592. Cowfold E,1433. C,1500. Etchingham M,1388. M,son,1444. 2W,1480,P. Firle M,W,1476. C,1595. G,1638. Fletching M,W,1380. Gloves, 1400. Grinstead, East 2M,1505. C,1520. Grinstead, West W,1440. M,W,1441. Horsham E,1411. W,1513. Hurstmonceux M,1402. Slaugham M,1503,P. M,3W,1547. W,1586. Stopham C,W,1460,1601,1462. M,W,1460. M,2W,1630. C,1630. Trotton W,1310. M,W,1421. Warbleton E,1436. Warminghurst C,W,1554. Wiston M,1426.

WARWICKSHIRE
Baginton M,W,1407. Coleshill E,1500. W,1506. C,1566. Coughton M,W,1535. Haseley M,W, 1573,P. Merevale M,W,1413. Middleton C,W,1476. Shuckburgh W,1500. M,W,1549,1594. Warwick, St. Mary M,W,1406. C,W,1573. Wellesbourne Hastings M,1426. Wixford M,W,1411. Ch,1597.

WESTMORELAND
Kendal C,1577. Musgrave, Great E,1500.

WILTSHIRE
Alton Priors W,1528. C,1620. Berwick Basset C,1427. Bradford-on-Avon C,W,1520. W,1601. Bromham W,1490. M,2W,1578. Cliffe-Pypard M,1380. Dauntsey M,W,1514. W,1539. Draycot Cerne M,W,1393. Fovant E,1500. Lacock M,W,1501. Mere M,1398,1425. Salisbury Cathedral E,1375,1576. Tisbury C,W,1520,1590. Wanborough C,W,1418. Westbury C,W,1605.

WORCESTERSHIRE
Daylesford C,1632. Fladbury M,W,1445. E,1458,1504. M,1488. Kidderminster M,W,1415. Strensham: M,1390,1405. M,W,1562. Tredington E,1427,1482. W,1561.

YORKSHIRE
Aldborough M,1360. Allerton Mauleverer M,W,1400. Beeford E,1472. Bolton-by-Bowland M,W,1520. Brandsburton E,1364. M,W,1397. Cottingham E,1383. C,W,1504. Cowthorpe C,1494. Doncaster C,1683,1699. Harpham M,W,1418. M,1445. Ilkley I,1562,P. C,1649,1671. Leeds, St. Peter M,W,1459. M,1467. E,1469. C,1709. Owston C,W,1409. Rawmarsh C,W,1616. Ripley E,1429. Routh M,W,1420. Sessay E,1550,P. Skipton-in-Craven M,1570. Sprotborough M,W,1474. Topcliffe C,W,1391,P. Wath C,W,1420. M,1490. Wensley E,1375. York: Minster E,1315. W,1585. C,1595. All Saints North Street C,1642. Symbols, etc, 1482. St. Martin, Coney Street C,1614. St. Michael, Spurriergate E,1466.

SCOTLAND
Aberdeen, St. Nich. C,1613. Glasgow M, 1605.

WALES
Anglesey: Beaumaris C,W,1530. Carnarvonshire: Dolwyddelan M,1525. Llanbeblig C,1500. Denbighshire: Llanrwst 6C brasses 1626–1671. Ruthin C,1560. C,W,1583. Whitchurch C,W,1575. Glamorganshire: Swansea C,W,1500. Montgomeryshire: Bettws, Newtown E,1531. Pembrokeshire: Haverfordwest C,W,1654.

BIBLIOGRAPHY

ARMS AND ARMOUR IN ENGLAND. Mann & Dufty. Pub. 1969 by H.M.S.O. A useful elementary guide to the subject of armour.

BEGINNERS GUIDE TO BRASS RUBBING. R. J. Busby. Pub. 1969 by Mayflower. Paperback for the beginner.

BRASSES. Julian Franklin. Pub. 1969 by Arco. Informative about brasses, but a little opinionated. First class chapter on reading inscriptions.

BRITISH MONUMENTAL BRASSES. Le Strange. Pub. 1972 Thames and Hudson. Very useful catalogue of all brasses. Mainly by counties.

BRASSES AND BRASS RUBBING IN ENGLAND. Jerome Bertram. Pub. 1971 by David & Charles. Excellent informative book about all aspects of subject.

DISCOVERING BRASSES. Malcolm Cook. Pub. by Shire Publications. Beginners handbook. Excellent.

BRASS RUBBING. Malcolm Norris. Pub. 1965 Studio Vista. Well illustrated book about British and Continental brasses.

THE CRAFT AND DESIGN OF MONUMENTAL BRASSES. Henry Trivick. Pub. 1969 by John Baker. Expensive lush book superbly illustrated, and full of information.

MONUMENTAL BRASSES. Macklin. Rewritten John Page Phillips. Pub. 1970 George Allen and Unwin. Classic on the subject. Excellent County lists and specially good information on dress and armour.

BRASS RUBBINGS. Victoria & Albert Museum. Pub. 1968 H.M.S.O. Indispensible catalogue with illustrations. Very easy to use. Some omissions.

INDEX

⚔ꝼꝛ Richard Attelese   1394

SIR RICHARD ATTELESE,
1394
Sheldwich, Kent. B.L.